ART QUILT
PORTFOLIO

The Natural World

Ruth B McDowell ©2008

ART QUILT
PORTFOLIO
The Natural World

PROFILES OF MAJOR ARTISTS

•

GALLERIES OF INSPIRING WORKS

Martha Sielman

LARK
CRAFTS
Asheville

EDITOR: **Valerie Van Arsdale Shrader**

ART DIRECTOR: **Megan Kirby**

DESIGNER: **Pamela Norman**

ART PRODUCTION: **Meagan Shirlen**

ASSISTANT EDITOR: **Thom O'Hearn**

EDITORIAL ASSISTANT: **Dawn Dillingham**

PRODUCTION EDITOR: **Julie Hale**

COVER DESIGNER: **Chris Bryant**

ON PAGE 2:
Ruth McDowell
Blue Clematis, 2008

FRONT COVER:
Barbara Barrick McKie
Peacock Pride, 2009

BACK COVER, CLOCKWISE FROM BOTTOM:
Elaine Quehl
Vagabond Song, 2010

Katherine K. Allen
Quiet Talk, 2010

Patricia Gould
Moonrise, North Rim, 2009

Cassandra Williams
Dance of the Deep, 2003

Barbara Barrick McKie
Mandarin Duck, 2010

Elaine Quehl
Unfurling, 2009

FRONT FLAP:
Judith Trager
Night Lilies, 2007

BACK FLAP:
Diane Marie Chaudiere
Lookout, 2009

Dottie Moore
The Call, 2009

SPINE:
Sally Scott
Axis Mundi Reflected, 2009

LARK CRAFTS

An Imprint of Sterling Publishing
387 Park Avenue South
New York, NY 10016

If you have questions or comments about
this book, please visit: larkcrafts.com

Library of Congress Cataloging-in-Publication Data

Sielman, Martha.
  Art quilt portfolio : the natural world : profiles of major artists, galleries of inspiring works / Martha Sielman. -- 1st ed.
      p. cm.
  Includes index.
  ISBN 978-1-60059-928-6
  1. Art quilts--United States--Themes, motives. 2. Nature in art. I. Title.
  NK9112.S497 2012
  746.46--dc23
                                    2011029983
  10 9 8 7 6 5 4 3 2 1

First Edition

Published by Lark Crafts
An Imprint of Sterling Publishing Co., Inc.
387 Park Avenue South, New York, NY 10016

Text © 2012, Martha Sielman
Photography © 2012, Artist/Photographer as specified

Distributed in Canada by Sterling Publishing,
c/o Canadian Manda Group, 165 Dufferin Street
Toronto, Ontario, Canada M6K 3H6

Distributed in the United Kingdom by GMC Distribution Services,
Castle Place, 166 High Street, Lewes, East Sussex, England BN7 1XU

Distributed in Australia by Capricorn Link (Australia) Pty Ltd.,
P.O. Box 704, Windsor, NSW 2756 Australia

ISBN 13: 978-1-60059-928-6

For information about custom editions, special sales, and premium and corporate purchases, please
contact Sterling Special Sales Department at 800-805-5489 or specialsales@sterlingpub.com.

For information about desk and examination copies available to college and university
professors, requests must be submitted to academic@larkbooks.com. Our complete policy
can be found at www.larkcrafts.com.

CONTENTS

INTRODUCTION

IN THE MID-1800s HENRY DAVID THOREAU FAMOUSLY WROTE, "in Wildness is the preservation of the World." This book is a celebration of that Wildness in all its forms—animals, rocks, flowers, trees, insects, and birds. The artists whose work is shown here are inspired to depict Wildness, studying it carefully and exploring it lovingly through the medium of the art quilt.

Many of my own favorite childhood memories involve time spent playing in the acre of woods surrounding my suburban home. I was convinced that fairies lived in the woods, and I sought them everywhere, finding many wonders of nature along the way. I marveled at the variety of golden colors found under the peeling bark of a white birch tree. I treasured the subtle palette and velvety softness of shelf fungus. I collected acorn cups for fairy dishes and tiny flowers for fairy décor.

I grew up near the Cold Spring Harbor Laboratory in Long Island, New York. They ran a summer camp for children that focused on studying nature, and I was an enthusiastic attendee. I learned to press leaves, to collect and mount insects, and to dissect grasshoppers and the mouse bones found in owl pellets. I added these collections to my ever-increasing piles of shoeboxes full of rocks, shells, and seaweeds collected on the Long Island beaches.

As a college student I took biology courses and studied bird migration patterns with my professor. In graduate school, I got a master's degree in museum education and did an internship at the Bronx Botanical Garden, as well as taking a year of graduate studies in biology at the University of Connecticut. I then worked for many years developing hands-on learning experiences for elementary school children in the sciences. I encouraged their teachers to give them the same types of experiences that I had had as a child, but I added such activities as looking at all the different types of rock present in a handful of sand, counting the repeating numbers of parts found in flower blossoms, and listening to the different sounds the wind makes when you stand among different types of trees.

During those years, my city-bred husband refered to me as "Nature Girl" and put up (fairly cheerfully) with dead chipmunks in the freezer, dried squirrel tails for the kids, and colonies of mealworms and crickets on the kitchen counters. While our menagerie has never been large, over the years it has included a rabbit, wood frogs, African clawed frogs, anole lizards, a variety of tropical fish, and, of course, cats.

My life-long love affair with nature is part of why I am excited that the theme of "The Natural World" is featured in the first volume of the new *Art Quilt Portfolio* series. The other reason is that the work being done on the subject of nature is incredibly varied and immensely compelling. The series is designed to showcase the best work being done on a particular theme. Gallery sections display the work of

PATRICIA GOULD ● COASTAL SYMPHONY, 2009 ● Photo by artist

more than 70 artists, while an in-depth treatment is given to a body of work created by 19 featured artists, showing several works by each, coupled with interviews describing their backgrounds and working methods.

When work began on this book, a call for entries was put out. Artwork was received from more than 450 artists. As I reviewed the images of almost 1,200 art quilts, I was amazed at the range and quality of work that is currently being done on the subject of nature. The next volume in the series will be *People and Portraits*, with additional volumes on abstract work, landscapes, and other topics planned to follow.

What links all of the artwork in this book—besides its subject matter—is the passion that these artists feel about the amazing diversity and indescribable beauty that they see in nature. The imagery may lean toward the abstract or be more realistic, but the artists all report feeling compelled to celebrate the world they see around them. Dottie Moore wrote, "Trees are my symbol for life, and I find messages in every one that I quilt." Ginny Eckley is fascinated by birds: "I feel birds mimic their surroundings. I love their songs and sounds, the combination of their movements...I love their nests, which in the city can be in signs, light posts, drain pipes—they are very resourceful."

One question that I asked each of the featured artists was how where they lived affected what they were drawn to create. Though they live in very different places, each artist is convinced that theirs is the best, most inspiring location. Katherine K. Allen responded, "The starkly differentiated lights and darks of South Florida present a world of shape, shadow, and silhouette that is abstracted in my work. Tropical sunlight influences the saturation of many of my color choices." Patricia Gould replied, "Since 1993 I have lived in New Mexico....After my husband and I moved [here], rocks become a major inspiration for my fiber art. The incredible skies here in the high desert are very strong influences on my work and enhance the beauty of the unique rock formations."

The artists featured in this book use a wide variety of techniques to capture the aspects of the natural world that fascinate them. Some artists, like Elaine Quehl, hand dye their own fabrics. Others, like Ruth McDowell, use only commercially available fabrics, and yet others, like Betty Busby, use preprinted fabrics that they then modify by over-dyeing and painting. Nancy Cook's seedpods are painted using transparent inks on whole-cloth backgrounds, while Sally Dillon's sea life studies start as separate silk paintings that she joins together. Many

MELANI KANE BREWER ● WALK IN THE WOODS I~CECROPIA, 2005 ● Photo by
Gerhard Heidersberger ● Collection of Judy Black and Richard Schlosberg, Florida

artists combine more than one process: Judith Trager combines pieced backgrounds with silk-screened floral studies, while Annemieke Mein uses a number of techniques, including all of the following in one particular piece: "...drawing, painting, dyeing, binding, plying, wiring, felting, padding, quilting, stuffing, molding, sculpting, layering and beading."

This volume also contains a group project. The Fiber Artists Coalition is a group of artists living in the upper Midwestern United States. They created a body of work inspired by Wallace Stevens' poem "Thirteen Ways of Looking at a Blackbird." Viewing works by 13 artists inspired by the same poem seemed to be a perfect metaphor for this book.

All of the artists in this volume are dedicated to creating with fiber. Dominie Nash argues that "the work would not be the same if it were not in fiber; there are qualities inherent in art made of fabric and thread: the particular depth of the colors, the layers, and the texture of the stitches, that can't be duplicated in another medium." Plus fiber has practical benefits, as pointed out by Ginny Smith: "Fabric as a medium does not require water, it is not toxic, it does not need to sit and dry, and conversely, it doesn't dry too fast. It is not heavy, it is readily available, and it can be easily manipulated. You can cut it, sew it, write on it, and make things that don't have to be on heavy stretchers or under glass. You can mail it in a tube, and it comes in more glorious colors and patterns than you could ever imagine. It is perfect, and I love it."

And finally, all of the artists in this volume wish to convey a heartfelt message about the importance of environmental stewardship, caring for the Earth we all share. Annie Helmericks-Louder wrote, "We have become the deadliest species on this planet. Our behavior toward other species—and this planet itself—indicates an almost total disregard for the sacredness, interconnectivity, and value of life." Melani Kane Brewer agrees: "Nature in all her glory surrounds us if we just care enough to look. How can we not be inspired by its beauty? From the tiniest spiders to the magnificent wood storks, from the translucent wings of the luna moth to the ancient cypress trees, these are nature's gifts...I hope in some small way that I am preserving nature in my fiber pieces for all to see and enjoy for eternity."

One definition of art is that it helps us to see things more clearly, to really pay attention to some aspect of the world around us—something that has always been there, but to which, in our busy lives, we haven't paid much attention. These artists and their artworks help us to see the worth and the wonder of the natural world. Whether we come face to face with the inner recesses of a flower in Paula Chung's works or marvel at the intricacies of a sea star in Karen Illman Miller's stencils, whether we are beguiled by the eyes of one of Cassandra Williams' giraffes or charmed by the mother and baby from one of Barbara Barrick McKie's pieces, we cannot view these artworks without becoming more aware of the beauty outside our own windows.

GINNY ECKLEY ● CERULEAN NEST IN TRUMPET VINES V, 2008 ● Photo by Rick Wells

JUDITH TRAGER

HER FLOWERS SEEM SO JOYOUS, DANCING IN THE SUN. Judith Trager's floral works celebrate the beauty of her beloved gardens now that she is no longer able to grow flowers herself. Each tulip, daylily, and sunflower is lovingly detailed and shaded. Her intricately pieced backgrounds provide the perfect foil for the flowers, as their rich colors shift and change across the surface, while a scattering of golden squares or some careful seed-stitch embroidery provides just the right accent. In contrast, her multi-piece installations are celebrations of the changing seasons, filled with wind-blown leaves chasing one another across the grandeur of the Colorado canyons. Trager has created works based on many different themes over the course of her career, but as she ages, she feels increasingly inspired to explore how the changes of the seasons reflect the seasons of her life.

SUNFLOWERS, 2009 ● 18 x 18 inches (45.7 x 45.7 cm) ●
Cotton, silk; machine quilted and pieced, direct appliquéd,
silk-screened ● Photo by Ken Sanville ● Private
collection of Dee Dee Rice, Boulder, Colorado

Family History

I was born in Paso Robles, California, on August 27, 1942, the night the Japanese shelled the beaches of San Luis Obispo County. My mother said she could hear the shelling. I was the thirteenth child in a 12-crib nursery, so I was put in a wooden orange crate, complete with its colorful label. To this day, I love orange crates and fresh oranges.

I am a child of the West. My father was a fourth-generation Californian steeped in the mysteries of the coastland. My mother was the daughter of Utah Mormon pioneers; everybody in her family knew how to sew and quilt. My mother had six sisters, and they all quilted, partly because they liked to talk, and they really dished when they sewed together around the quilting frame. It was just amazing. I heard gossip about the family that I would never have heard if I hadn't been a little kid who was fascinated by quilting. My mother came from a family of 14 children, and I have 96 first cousins.

NIGHT LILIES, 2007 ● 24 x 24 inches (61 x 61 cm) ● Cotton, silk; machine quilted and pieced, direct appliquéd, silk-screened ● Photo by Ken Sanville

The West

I have always been drawn to wild places and find the drama and color of the West essential to my well-being. My work is heavily driven by my surroundings—the aspen trees through the seasons, the colors of the Flatirons Mountains in the dawn, the ancient cliffs of the Canyonlands. I have lived for the past 25 years in Colorado. It is heaven on earth.

When we lived in the Midwest and the East, it was very hard for me to create at the same scale and with the same power I do now. I felt smothered by trees. I missed the openness of the sky and the contrast of the rugged landscape. My work was not very good, so to make up for it, I fell back on traditional patterns and designs.

Power of Cloth

I believe in the power of cloth. It is essential to humans on a daily basis for covering, warmth, and ornamentation. It also defines who we are and tells the rest of the world what we think. No other medium has that power for me. I am happiest when using cloth to make objects that stretch the viewer's imagination, making the audience think in a new dimension about how this homely material can be at once simple and powerful. Although I have a fine arts degree and have puttered around with other disciplines—painting and ceramics—I always return to fiber as my base. It is primal for me. When we are born, the first thing that happens to us is that we are wrapped in cloth, swaddled in a blanket. We will be wrapped in cloth when we die, ceremonially taking our bodies and spirits to another place.

HARBINGER, 2008 ● 41 x 56 inches (104.1 x 142.2 cm) ● Cotton, silk; machine quilted and pieced, direct appliquéd, silk-screened ● Photo by Ken Sanville ● Collection of St. Joseph Mercy Hospital, Ypsilante, Michigan

Drawing

I very strongly advise the beginning quilter to take a drawing class. Don't think of yourself in terms of being able to draw or not being able to draw; it is the experience and discipline of doing it that is important. Even though I had studied painting in college, when I went back to get my MFA I discovered that drawing helps you organize and clarify your vision. Drawing is just a skill anybody can learn. You don't need talent, because I have none. Drawing gives you a way of seeing.

Steps in the Process

It begins with ideas: Often immediate, sometimes found on the edges of sleep and needing a bit of coaxing to develop. I carry a small sketchbook or journal with me wherever I go, and I sometimes take photographs.

In the design phase I work with paper and colored pencils to make a rough cartoon. In assessing my palette I see what I have on my shelves that can bring the idea to life, and I paint additional background fabrics.

STARGAZERS, 2009 ● 14 x 19 inches (35.6 x 48.3 cm) ● Cotton, silk; machine quilted and pieced, direct appliquéd, silk-screened ● Photo by Ken Sanville ● Collection of Christina Tomlinson, Washington, DC

CALYPSO, 2009 ● 22 x 31 inches (55.9 x 78.7 cm) ● Cotton, silk; machine quilted and pieced, direct appliquéd, silk-screened ● Photo by Ken Sanville

I cut out shapes freehand with a rotary cutter and then assemble the background blocks, messing about with colors to see what works. I do all the silk-screening for a particular piece right on top of the sewn blocks, using thin acrylic inks and paints.

I use fabric glue to assemble the layers, placing a standard 80/20 cotton/polyester batting and a cotton or linen backing fabric that matches the colors of the front.

During the first quilting pass I outline the silk-screened images and then I dry-brush paint for light-and-shadow effects. I use fusibles to do direct appliqué right over the existing quilting/silk screening. During the second quilting pass I add more finished quilting, noting the importance of pattern.

At the hand-embroidery phase I almost always add seed stitches with DMC embroidery floss. Because I am unable to use small needles any longer, I hire someone to do the final hemstitching for me.

I sign the quilt in front and create a label for the back. Then I have the quilt professionally photographed before it goes anywhere.

Geometric Backgrounds

The geometric blocks I use in my backgrounds are in large part a tribute to the traditional quilters who came before me. They also allow me to add variety in color and textures. I am able to superimpose natural elements and images on top of them, much like a garden is built around a wall. I like the idea of being able to control the environment, even though I know that sense of control is illusory.

Work in a Series

Beginning in 1991, I started on a series called *Plastic Flowers in a Mexican Graveyard*, a body of work of about 25 pieces. When I was a child, between the ages of four and 16, I lived in Mexico. My parents were part-time

EQUINOX, 2008 ● 36 x 144 inches (91.4 x 365.8 cm) ● Cotton, silk; machine quilted and pieced, direct appliquéd, silk-screened ● Photo by Ken Sanville ● Collection of Marla and John Simmet, St. Paul, Minnesota

expats right after the war, and we ran a fishing resort, really a camp, in Baja, California. I fell in love with Mexico. It took me until I was in my 50s to really be able to express the colors and the feelings of that experience. That series was my first one-woman traveling show; one piece from that show, *Lost Childhood*, was purchased by the American Folk Art Museum.

I was later invited by the curator of the American Craft Museum to do a show at the Chautauqua Gallery in Chautauqua, New York. I did a four-piece series called *Lake Effect*, which became the start of my series on the seasons. I later made a piece called *September*, which grew out of a desire to show how everything happens at once in that month. It is still summer but that is when the leaves begin to change to their autumn colors. I'm also getting older, so I'm interested in how my life is changing. How the colors change from greens and reds to golds is both physical and metaphorical.

I always work on more than one series at a time, but each piece builds upon the one before. One piece always informs my work for the next piece.

Keep Working

I had been an avid gardener until about 2004 or 2005, when I discovered that I could no longer do the physical work. So I started making garden quilts. I had already been working on my series about the seasons, but I began to turn my seasonal quilts into garden quilts, quilts with big flowers and all sorts of big plants.

Now I tell people: Don't ever stop working. Whatever your circumstances are, don't stop making art. If you are challenged and can no longer physically make what you made at one time, find another way of working, find another way to make art. It can be as simple as making tiny little things or drawing or learning to watercolor. It is important to keep doing it, because it keeps you alive.

PAULA CHUNG

IN ONE PETAL OF AN IRIS IMAGE by Paula Chung, there are 12 colors of silk, maybe more. The iris is slowly withering, its time in the sun complete, but Chung's portraits of its progress demonstrate just how much beauty there can be in the process of aging. She sees her flowers as metaphors for her life. Working exclusively in raw-edge appliqué and hand-dyed silks, her works start with photographic realism, which she then simplifies until the images appear almost abstract. The flower's center becomes a microcosm; its carefully rendered colors and shapes are enlarged until we almost forget that they are just a part of a flower. Myriad shades and sensuous forms interact to create a sinuous beauty. As Chung's work shows, there is a continuous dramatic cycle of life and death in the flower garden.

WILD ARTICHOKE V, 2009 ● 54 x 72 inches (137.2 x 182.9 cm)
● Hand-dyed silk; machine appliquéd, machine quilted ●
Photo by artist

Second Career

I began quilting in the early 1970s as a hobby, using the old tried-and-true methods: hand tracing templates and hand sewing all the little pieces into blocks, then hand quilting the whole piece. Although I enjoyed the pattern and color manipulation, knowing the outcome of the piece before it was completed eventually lost its appeal.

When we retired from our careers and moved to Lake Tahoe in northern Nevada, it definitely affected my life and the way I see the world. Living in such beautiful surroundings in a rural area has allowed me to live with and appreciate nature. And having the opportunity to finally study art and pursue an art degree has allowed me to explore new ways to express myself. I think if I had not moved to Lake Tahoe and studied sculpture, drawing, and painting, I would not have started in this new direction.

AGING IRIS IV, 2010 ● 84 x 64 inches (213.4 x 162.6 cm) ● Hand-dyed silk; machine appliquéd, machine quilted ● Photo by artist

Flowers

I use flowers to mimic life—from birth to death. I guess as I'm aging, I'm having flowers tell my story as well. I have always been an enthusiastic gardener and now have gardens in the High Sierras and in a coastal region of Southern California. Having two gardens presents lots of problems, but it gives me great diversity.

My gardens provide a never-ending source of inspiration and solace. Flowers, especially, speak to me. My pieces try to capture their essence, their energy, and the awe I feel when experiencing their beauty. Photographs and drawings enable me to capture with my fiber art what the flower says to me. It is a very personal message that I hope to convey.

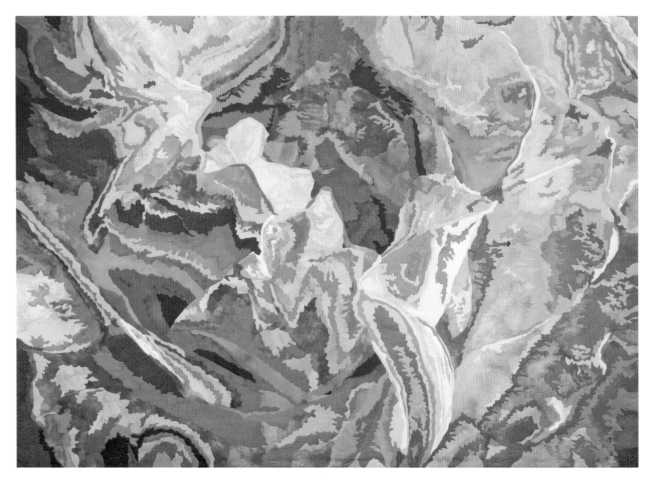

DARK ROSE V, 2008 ● 54 x 70 inches (137.2 x 177.8 cm) ● Hand-dyed silk; machine appliquéd, machine quilted ● Photo by artist

Color

My art quilts are made of hand- or commercially dyed silks. I often over-dye the silk many times to capture a fuller, richer depth of color. I'd like to say that my environment influences my palette, but I think that it's just my state of mind at the time. In my *Dark Rose* series, I found that my colors were more somber and realized I had mapped out the colors when my dad was ill and dying. Others reflect a happier time, with bright, vibrant colors. My most recent series have more complex colors, reflecting my aging process and mourning the loss of dear friends.

JAPANESE ANEMONE I, 2007 ● 52 x 88 inches (132.1 x 223.5 cm) ● Hand-dyed silk; machine appliquéd, machine quilted ● Photo by artist

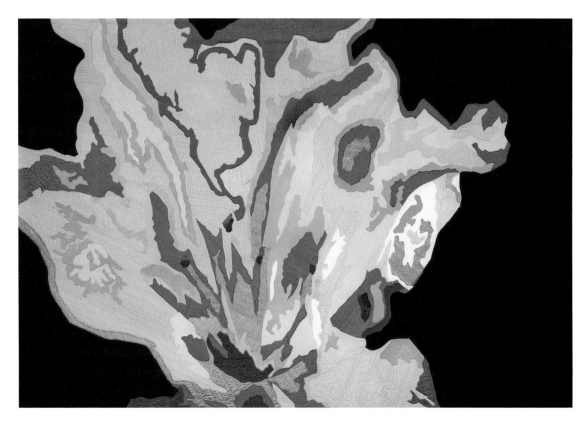

WHITE AZALEA III, 2006 ● 25 x 35 inches (63.5 x 88.9 cm) ● Hand-dyed silk; machine appliquéd, machine quilted ● Photo by artist

Painting with Fiber

I photograph a subject and manipulate it in Photoshop. I print the photo onto regular paper and create a map of the colors and values I want to use. I dye silk in the colors I need for the project if I don't already have the right colors and values.

After I trace the image, adding codes that I've developed to indicate color and value, I enlarge it with an overhead projector. I make a master drawing from that image and then trace that master (backwards) onto butcher paper, which becomes the pattern for the pieces. After adding another code to tell me the position of each piece, I cut the pieces out. Then I begin cutting the fabric. I back the silk with fusible interfacing to make it easier to handle and less likely to fray.

I work in segments, cutting and placing the pieces temporarily, lightly tacking the pieces together using an archival glue stick. I stitch the sections together raw edged, using monofilament thread with a tiny zigzag stitch. When all the segments are completed, I work out any design problems by pinning them up onto my design wall and moving them around. Then I sew the segments together.

I attach a cotton/poly batting and machine quilt densely, either following the contour lines or in a random wavy pattern. I block the quilt, square it up, and add a pillowcase-edge binding with hand-dyed cotton sheeting.

Why Fiber?

Although I love sculpting and painting, I find fiber has a broader spectrum of techniques and applications. We can create two- or three-dimensional forms. The ability to manipulate fiber in so many ways is what makes it exciting. I had an early affinity for fiber, having sewn since I was a child.

I only work with silk fabrics. Silk has many differing textures and different responses to light, both absorbing and reflecting it. Silk has a formidable presence and history, and I try to honor that.

Georgia O'Keeffe

I think Georgia O'Keeffe has influenced me in a lot of different ways. My first introduction to her was several decades ago. I admired her use of color and subject matter. Now that I've had the opportunity to study art in greater depth, I appreciate her use of value, the contrast of hard and soft edges in her work, and her dramatic use of color. It is very difficult to make something simple, to remove all the unnecessary information. O'Keeffe is a master at simplification, and she creates images of sweeping beauty to tell her stories of life, death, and love.

This series of garden quilts began with some intriguing photos I took of tulips in the spring of 2005. I was so taken by their stunning colors and forms. My first pieces were very primitive, without a good sense of form, value, or color. Over time, my quilts have become more stylized, letting the colors and shapes tell the story. I recall a statement by Georgia O'Keeffe describing her choice of subjects in 1926. The flowers fascinated her so much that she forgot what they were except that they were shapes together. I hope that I am capturing those incredible shapes that I see within a blossom and the amazing subtlety of their colors.

Interpreting Nature

I am endeavoring to interpret my feelings in my images of flowers: some common, some exotic. I strive not to duplicate nature but to convey it as I envision it. I strive to show its beauty, strength, and vulnerability through my work. As O'Keeffe said about her large flower paintings: Stop and experience the beauty of flowers.

WHITE ROSE XI, 2007 ● 48 x 64 inches (121.9 x 162.6 cm) ● Hand-dyed silk; machine appliquéd, machine quilted ● Photo by artist

flowers I

FRIEDA ANDERSON ● WOODLAND SECRETS, 2010 ● 43 x 43 inches (109.2 x 109.2 cm) ●
Cotton and silk; hand dyed, machine appliquéd, machine quilted ● Photo by artist

ANDREA M. BROKENSHIRE ● JEANENE'S SWEETIE PEAS, 2010 ● 40 x 29 x ¼ inches (101.6 x 73.7 x 0.6 cm)
100% silk, 100% cotton; hand-painted appliqué, free-motion machine quilted ● Photo by artist

MAIJA BRUMMER ● PRIMAVERA, 2005 ● 40 x 40 x ³/₁₆ inches (101.6 x 101.6 x 0.5 cm) ● 100% cotton surface and backing; hand dyed, hand painted, free-motion machine embroidered ● Photo by Sirpa Pollanen

GEORGIE CLINE ● WHOLE I: YELLOW FLOWERS I,
2004 ● 39 x 29 inches (99.1 x 73.7 cm) ●
Cotton- and silk-blend commercial and hand-dyed
fabric, tulle, acrylic paint, metallic fabric paint;
machine appliquéd ● Photo by artist

DEBRA DANKO ● PINK ORCHID, 2006 ● 36 x 49 inches (91.4 x 124.5 cm) ● Cotton fabrics, shibori cotton fabric, cotton batting; painted, fused, hand dyed, machine quilted ● Photo by artist

RUTH DE VOS ● SOLOMON..., 2007 ● 58½ x 71⁷⁄₁₆ inches (148.6 x 181.5 cm) ● 100% cotton, dye; hand dyed, machine pieced, machine quilted ● Photo by Victor France

MELINDA BULA ● RAIN DROPS, 2010 ● 23 x 25 inches (58.4 x 63.5 cm) ● 100% cotton fabrics (some hand dyed by the artist), rayon thread; thread painted, fusible appliqué ● Photo by artist

DEBRA DANKO ● BIG PETUNIAS, 2005 ●
39 x 52 inches (99.1 x 132.1 cm) ● Cotton
fabrics, layered silk organza, cotton batting;
painted, machine appliquéd, hand dyed,
machine embroidered, machine quilted ●
Photo by artist

PAMELA ALLEN ● ODD GARDEN, 2010 ●
43 x 43 inches (109.2 x 109.2 cm) ● Cotton
and silk; hand dyed, machine appliquéd,
machine quilted ● Photo by artist

● Flowers I

GINNY SMITH

WE IDENTIFY WITH BIRDS, PERHAPS BECAUSE they also have two legs. Perched together or flying as a flock, they seem to mirror our society. Birds are often viewed as wise, all-seeing, messengers from the gods. Ginny Smith's birds can be raucous, aggressive, or melancholy, but they always seem to be trying to convey a message of some importance. They are clearly telling part of a mysterious story, which we attempt to interpret, wondering what has happened, and what will happen next. Influenced by her study of historic textiles, Smith's birds are often accompanied by classic urns and flowers, yet they have an energy and power that their historical antecedents lack. They bring us sage advice—will we heed it?

OISEAUX FOUS, 2008 ● 76 x 74 inches (193 x 188 cm) ●
100% cotton; machine pieced, appliquéd, and quilted ●
Photo by Steve Tuttle

Why Fiber?

I use fabric and thread for several reasons. I do not come from a sewing background but rather from a fine art background. Fabric was one of many media I used in art school, and afterward, when I had children, its benefits were unmistakable. Fabric doesn't require water. It isn't toxic, and it doesn't need to sit and dry. Conversely, it doesn't dry too fast. It isn't heavy, and it's readily available. It can be easily manipulated. You can cut it, sew it, write on it, and make things that don't have to be on heavy stretchers or under glass. You can mail it in a tube, and it comes in more glorious colors and patterns than you could ever imagine. It's perfect, and I love it.

Fine Art Background

I currently live in Arlington, Virginia. I've been in the Washington, D.C., area since 1969. I went to art school here and learned to quilt here. I became an artist using fiber here, learning from friends and from the world-class art that's in the capital area. Going to art school here was probably an important factor in my art making and also seeing the touring show "Abstract Design in American Quilts" at the Renwick Gallery of the Smithsonian, which demonstrated the expressive power of traditional quilts and the consummate artistry possible in quilt-making.

ANXIETY WON, 2006 ● 68¾ x 62½ inches (174.6 x 158.8 cm) ● 100% cotton; hand appliquéd, machine pieced, hand quilted ● Photo by Steve Tuttle

BIRD, 2006 ● 19½ x 26 inches (49.5 x 66 cm) ● 100% cotton; hand appliquéd, quilted, and embroidered ● Photo by Steve Tuttle

ORIGINAL SIN, 2008 ● 34¼ x 45½ inches (87 x 115.6 cm) ● 100% cotton; machine pieced, appliquéd, and quilted ● Photo by Steve Tuttle

Inspiration

I draw inspiration from many diverse sources, from quilts—old, odd, energetic quilts with uncomfortable color combinations and eccentric stitching—to historical textiles such as holy relics, quilted armor, and story-telling embroideries. Important influences are contemporary artists such as Elizabeth Murray, Anselm Kiefer, and Frank Stella. I often revisit old favorites like Joseph Cornell and Henri Rousseau. I especially enjoy folk and so-called outsider art—lately, the pencil drawings of Martin Ramirez. Finally, I draw upon the natural world, and the myths, legends, and folktales we have devised to explain that world.

Birds

The bird is a common image in traditional quilts and needlework. Birds are found in cultures all over the world. They're thought to be symbolic of many things: They're guardians of nations, able to fly and see the earth from above, and thus to see the Truth. Birds in all their variety make great subjects to draw, to abstract. There are so many variables to birds that it is easy to make your own. Mine is a blackish-blue, stooped, old, kind of vaguely crow-like bird; or a bird that wears a bowler hat, or that tells the future. Given the actual world of birds that you can draw from, making your own birds is a walk in the park.

Once you have made a bird, it seems natural to find a reason for its existence. On old quilts, birds often flank an urn of appliquéd flowers. Are they just decorative, or are they guardians? Or watchers? Are they symptoms or causes? The stories don't need to be told, but they need to inform the work and the decisions that go into making the work. My birds fit into a framework that is still under construction. The quilts offer glimpses of this fictional world but do not explain it. That comes further down the line.

Learning How to Look

What I learned at art school was how to look at the world in a profoundly basic way as a gigantic source of images and inspiration. The world gives me a pigeon wheeling in the sky, and I make flocks of birds as a commentary on modern life. I do a lot of drawing, subjective drawing with only a tenuous tie to representation. I draw all the time, and after a while certain compositions become important, and I focus on them. Sometimes I use a gridded cartoon and enlarge the image, which I then appliqué onto a background. I usually work on the background in roughly block-like shapes and raw-edge appliqué the birds on that. Currently, I am in the process of trying to find a way to make large pieces without too much preliminary work, because too much preliminary work seems to take the life out of the subject matter. My methods are pretty much old-school: using the back door as a light table and enlarging with a grid.

AVIARY, 2010 ● 45 x 63¼ inches (114.6 x 160.6 cm) ● 100% cotton; machine pieced, appliquéd, and quilted ● Photo by Steve Tuttle

Cameras and Computers

I take lots of photos, especially of pigeons. This is so I can see how they're put together, not so I'll have images to copy. I don't work from photographs, but rather from my drawings. I have a computer that I use for writng and looking at photos but I don't use it to make art, because I haven't found the need.

Color Choices

The color choices lately have been very simple; if you color the birds dark blue, then it seems logical to make the background caustic yellow, making the value difference as strong as it can be. It is not a subtle choice, but it increases the impact of the birds. I would be happy if, after seeing my work, people looked at birds more carefully and thought about their place in the world.

The Sayings on the Pieces

I make them up. Some of the quilts need words; some don't. The words speak to the quilt but are also graphic decorations chosen to fit into particular spaces and to enhance various aspects of the pieces. I react to the world by creating my own characters, who act where I cannot and fight back when I am fearful.

NIGHT WOODS, 2007 ● 67½ x 59½ inches (171.5 x 151.2 cm) ● 100% cotton; machine pieced and appliquéd, hand quilted ● Photo by Steve Tuttle

SANCTUARY, 2007 ● 43½ x 29½ inches (110.5 x 75 cm) ● 100% cotton; machine pieced and appliquéd, hand quilted ● Photo by Steve Tuttle

THIRTEEN WAYS OF LOOKING AT A BLACKBIRD

THE FIBER ARTISTS COALITION (FAC) IS A GROUP OF ARTISTS living in the upper midwestern United States. FAC curates exhibits of its members' contemporary fiber art and arranges for the exhibits to travel throughout the Midwest and beyond. Members of the group share their reflections on this project below.

FRIEDA ANDERSON ● IN THE FIELD, 2010 ● 22 x 25 inches (55.8 x 63.5 cm) ● Cotton fabrics; hand dyed ● Photo by artist

Inspiration

Member Clairan Ferrono proposed this themed exhibit to the group. "Looking at our work, I thought that something from the natural world would embrace our different artistic styles and create a cohesive show. My background and education are in literature, and I love poetry. I had been working individually on a series based on a poem, so my thoughts turned to one of my favorite poets, Wallace Stevens, and his beautiful and complex poem 'Thirteen Ways of Looking at a Blackbird.' The poem is long, but spare, full of wonderful natural imagery, but enigmatic. I asked the FAC members to read the poem and let me know if they'd like to respond to it, use it as inspiration for one to three pieces of work. Everyone was quite enthusiastic. I think the strength and beauty of this exhibit reveals one of the poem's deeper meanings—everyone's perception is different, but the mystery and promise of nature are eternal."

Frieda Anderson
In the Field

I live in the Midwest, a land of endless farm fields and rolling landscapes. Traveling along these roads and highways, my eyes wander over the patterned terrain, and my gaze is irresistibly drawn further and further to that distant horizon. Often I see the crows, sitting in the fields, reaping the rewards of our hard labor.

Astrid Hilger Bennett
The Beauty of Innuendo

Wallace Stevens' poem suggests physical experiences and mystical interpretations of the natural world. Interpreting stanza V, I acknowledged the temporary, fleeting nature of a blackbird, now whistling, now in the empty space of sound just after the whistle. Whistling suggests inflection, or the variation of words and sound. Absence of whistling or space suggests innuendo, a promise of what could be. What speaks best to me, the beauty of inflection or the beauty of innuendo? I do not know. The question hangs in a quiet, abstract balance.

ASTRID HILGER BENNETT ● THE BEAUTY OF INNUENDO, 2010 ●
60 x 38 inches (152.4 x 96.5 cm) ● 100% cotton fabrics, needle-punched
cotton batting; hand painted, monoprinted ● Photo by artist

Kathie Briggs

On November Winds

A single line in the poem, "When the blackbird flew out of sight," inspired *On November Winds*. Always fascinated by birds, I often watch them and wonder where they are going; do they have a destination in mind or do they let the wind guide them? Although they are around us all year, they seem to be in their glory in late autumn, cawing loudly as they ride winds above the bare trees and leaves swirl around them.

KATHIE BRIGGS ● ON NOVEMBER WINDS, 2009 ●
17½ x 23½ inches (44.5 x 59.7 cm) ● Hand-dyed and commercial cotton fabric, beads; machine pieced, appliquéd, and quilted, hand beaded ● Photo by artist

Kathie Briggs

The 13th Blackbird

The thirteenth and final stanza in the poem describes the quintessential winter day in northern Michigan, where we often have "evening all afternoon." If it isn't already snowing, the air seems heavy with imminent snowfall. The birds are quiet. They have found refuge in the evergreens. On those snowy days the only colors that interrupt the snow are the gray of the sky, the darker gray of the tree trunks, and the green needles of the conifers. Although darker than his surroundings, the blackbird in the cedar is nearly invisible in the fading light. Only the glint of his eye shows he's not part of the permanent landscape.

KATHIE BRIGGS ● THE 13TH BLACKBIRD, 2009 ●
27½ x 27 inches (69.9 x 68.6 cm) ● Hand-dyed and commercial cotton fabrics, red bead; machine pieced, appliquéd, and quilted, hand beaded ● Photo by artist

Shelley Brucar

Interesting Color for a Blackbird

There is a line in stanza X that refers to blackbirds "flying in a green light," which brought to mind the image of *black* birds with *green* feathers. It is my hope that the viewer will let go of the demands of daily life and step into that moment with me.

SHELLEY BRUCAR ● INTERESTING COLOR FOR A BLACKBIRD, 2009 ●
36 x 22 inches (91.4 x 55.9 cm) ● 100% cotton; hand dyed and screened,
appliquéd, machine stitched ● Photo by artist

Cheryl Dineen Ferrin
Blackbirds at Her Feet #1 and #2

The poem is masterful in its minimalism. I was particularly moved by stanza VII, where Stevens admonishes men grasping for wealth and materialism to see the true value in life. The blackbird in this stanza is enlightenment itself and shows them the way. The images this stanza created in my mind were vivid; I wanted to distill my vision in the same way the poet had. My distilled vision became blackbirds and women, existing in a shimmering surface of hand-dyed silk with the depth of black silk noil.

CHERYL DINEEN FERRIN ● BLACKBIRDS AT HER FEET #1, 2009 ● 70 x 50 inches (177.8 x 127 cm) ● 100% cotton; hand appliquéd, machine pieced, hand quilted ● Photo by artist

CHERYL DINEEN FERRIN ● BLACKBIRDS AT HER FEET #2, 2009 ● 70 x 50 inches (177.8 x 127 cm) ● 100% cotton; hand appliquéd, machine pieced, hand quilted ● Photo by artist

Clairan Ferrono
Eye of the Blackbird

I believe the theme of Stevens' poem is perception. In *Eye of the Blackbird*, the literal bird's eye is the focus of the piece in a whited-out world. What does it see?

Clairan Ferrono
Three Minds

In *Three Minds* I brought the blackbird into a brooding cityscape. Is the blackbird free or isolated? Or both?

CLAIRAN FERRONO ● THREE MINDS, 2009 ●
17 x 14½ inches (43.2 x 36.9 cm) ● Cotton duck, cheesecloth, gesso, thread, paper, ink, paint; printed, painted, collaged ●
Photo by Gerald Reuter

CLAIRAN FERRONO ●
EYE OF THE BLACKBIRD, 2009 ●
36½ x 11½ inches (92.7 x 29.2 cm)
● Cotton duck, cheesecloth, lace, wool roving, gesso, paper, ink, paint gel medium; needle felted, collaged, painted ● Photo by Gerald Reuter

Peg Keeney
13 Blackbirds

I tried to interpret Stevens' sense of the mystical forces in the dance of life. His haiku-like wording called for a simple but sensuous presentation, while the third and fourth stanzas provided specific guideposts. The blackbird is "everyman."

PEG KEENEY ● 13 BLACKBIRDS, 2009 ● 39½ x 32 inches (100.4 x 81.3 cm) ● Silk, cotton, metallic thread, cotton thread, silk thread; silk-screened, raw-edge appliquéd, free-motion quilted ● Photo by artist

Pat Kroth
Wingspeak

The section of the poem that I selected, stanza II, resonated with me:

"I was of three minds,
Like a tree
In which there are three blackbirds."

As a parent raising four children, I have often found myself of three or four or more minds, moving in different directions, playing, problem solving, cajoling, mentoring, instructing, consoling....

Blackbirds have unique verbal, physical, and poetic languages. They often visit near my studio window, chattering, calling to each other in a specific language of voice and posture, which is entirely their own.

PAT KROTH ● WINGSPEAK, 2009
54 x 18 inches (137.2 x 45.7 cm) ●
Hand-dyed cotton and mixed-content fabrics, nylon tulle, polyester, cotton, wool, synthetic fibers, fibers; machine stitched ● Photo by artist

BJ Parady

Blackbird Moon

For this piece, I was exploring the shape of a bird—how simple can a shape be and still read instantly to the viewer as "bird?" At the same time, I have been including a circle in my pieces that to me symbolizes the new moon that sometimes can be seen in the daytime. Even though the sun is not hitting it directly, it still has a visible presence in the sky.

BJ Parady

Green Skies

The background is acrylic paint poured on unprimed canvas. Even though the sky turned out to be an unusual color, I was very interested in developing the piece into an art quilt. Then along came the blackbird challenge...and when I read the poem, I noticed a line about green skies, and that was that. Once again, the shape of the blackbird is only suggestive of a bird. He (and in my mind it is a he) is made of silk scrim, and thus becomes less important than the sky he observes.

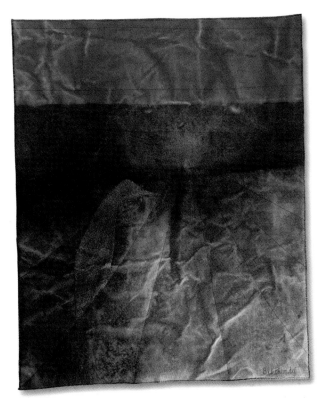

BJ PARADY ● GREEN SKIES, 2010 ● 22 x 17½ x ½ inches (55.9 x 44.5 x 1.3 cm) ● Canvas, silk scrim; painted, machine quilted ● Photo by artist

BJ PARADY ● BLACKBIRD MOON, 2009 ● 28 x 13 x ½ inches (71.1 x 33 x 3.8 cm) ● Silks, cotton; dyed, fused, machine quilted ● Photo by artist

Joan Potter Thomas
The River

I had been playing with black-and-white images in my work for a while. When I read the stanza about the river (VII), I knew that a solid blackbird over a running river would allow me to continue to explore a black-and-white theme. The challenge was drawing the blackbird with no shading so it looked like it was flying. I had to experiment quite a bit before I got a realistic silhouette. I decided to loosely stipple-quilt the entire piece, mimicking the churning effect of the water.

Laura Wasilowski
Colleen's Calling Birds #13

The reality we see is really a product of our imagination. With imagination we deal with everyday life and create an ever-changing world.

LAURA WASILOWSKI ● COLEEN'S CALLING BIRDS #13, 2009 ● 12 x 13 inches (30.4 x 33 cm) ● Hand-dyed 100% silk, pearl cotton thread; fused appliqué, hand embroidered ● Photo by artist

JOAN POTTER THOMAS ● THE RIVER, 2009 ● 34 x 22 inches (86.4 x 55.9 cm) ● 100% hand-dyed and commercial cotton; fused, machine quilted ● Photo by artist

Casey Puetz

Bird's-Eye View

Stevens noted 13 ways to look at blackbirds. The number 13 seemed a bit unlucky to me...so I used the number seven as a more welcoming figure. I created one large eye, containing the reflection of one blackbird, which is looking at six other blackbirds perched in trees. The activity of the birds appears to be a search for the sparkling crystals scattered throughout the piece. Curiosity is a curious thing.

CASEY PUETZ ● BIRD'S-EYE VIEW, 2009 ● 14 x 35⅜ inches (35.6 x 89.9 cm) ●
100% cotton, crystals; fused, silk-screened, raw-edge fused appliqué, machine quilted ●
Photo by William Lemke

Trish Williams

Where Two or More...

Where Two or More... was inspired by stanza III:

> "The blackbird whirled in the autumn winds.
> It was a small part of the pantomime."

TRISH WILLIAMS ● WHERE TWO OR MORE... , 2007 ● 24 x 35 inches
(61 x 88.9 cm) ● African kente cloth, hand-dyed cottons, Ultrasuede, commercial
cotton; machine pieced, quilted, embroidered, hand drawn ● Photo by artist

GINNY ECKLEY

A FASCINATION WITH NATURE, ESPECIALLY BIRDS AND FISH of all species, leads Ginny Eckley to create art that explores how these creatures live and interact. Whether it's the life cycle of a salmon struggling to return to its birthplace to spawn and lay its eggs, or discovering how cowbirds trick yellow warbler parents into raising their interloping young, Eckley is fascinated by the natural world and driven to convey the results of her careful research through fabric art. Using a variety of techniques—screen-printing, airbrushing, color washes, inkjet printing, and machine embroidery—she portrays schools of koi swimming through the water, flowers blooming in the desert, and birds raising their nestlings. Her recent **City Birds** series presents a different view of the natural world, with flocks of grackles perching on telephone wires or congregating on city buildings. These birds have successfully adapted to unnatural environments, making new use of manmade landscapes.

GATED COMMUNITY VIII, 2009 ● 42 x 42 x ½ inches (106.7 x 106.7 x 1.3 cm) ● Silks; silk-screened, hand painted, machine embroidered, machine quilted ● Photo by Rick Wells

First Memory of Sewing

I was eight years old, living in Mount Healthy, Ohio, and a neighbor lady, Mrs. Korn, was on her front porch sewing. I was so fascinated and interested. I just kept coming back every day, until she finally said, "Do you want to learn how to sew?" She taught me how to hand sew over the summer. After learning the basic stitches, we made a dress. When it was finished, I was so excited to take it home. When I showed my mom and brothers the dress, my brothers laughed and called it a muumuu. After that I decided I couldn't wear it, but I knew how to sew from that point on.

Quilting

My grandmother could knit, crochet, and sew beautifully. As I grew up, we created together. Near the end of her life, I made dresses for her that she had designed. She also grew roses, and I embroidered one of her dresses with drawings I made of her roses. From early on, I combined a love of nature with a love of creating.

CITY BIRDS VI, 2009 ● 35 x 32 inches (88.9 x 81.3 cm) ● 100% silks; hand painted, silk-screened, free-motion quilted ●
Photo by Rick Wells

WARBLER IN AUTUMN, 2008 ● 14 x 11 inches
(35.6 x 27.9 cm) ● Silks; hand painted, free-motion
embroidered ● Photo by Rick Wells

CERULEAN NEST IN TRUMPET VINES V, 2008 ●
28 x 22 x 1 inches (71.1 x 55.9 x 2.5 cm) ● Silks; hand
painted, free-motion embroidered ● Photo by Rick Wells

In the 1970s I made some pretty wild bedspreads. I did "layering." It probably was quilting by today's standards, but by 1970s standards I don't think these would have been called quilts. The word quilt applied only to traditional patchwork designs, so I never even thought of the word quilt when I was making these bedspreads.

I started art quilting in 1986, when my daughter was little. I had been working in an interior design shop, but I was tired of matching colors for people. I wanted to make something where I could put my own colors in and not have to match a couch or tile floor. I wanted to put something on the wall. Since my daughter was a really active kid, I needed to do something small, so I started doing small quilts. My first pieces were based on the amazing characteristics of fish.

Working in Fabric

I think that what I really enjoy the most is the fact that I am working on fabric. I love that fabric can conform to a shape. My earliest creations were clothing for myself and dolls. In college, I made sculpture with it. I also love the history of fabric. Knowing cotton fabric was created from plants and woven gives it more meaning for me. Instead of being a flat, stiff canvas, it has suppleness and texture. I feel I can do anything with it.

I do experiment a lot. When I have an idea for a piece, I'll spend weeks drawing and researching, and then I'll do small pieces where I paint my idea to see if it's going to work.

Art Degree

I have a degree in art, but it was difficult to achieve. I was enrolled in a college in upstate New York when my father was transferred to Texas. Since my parents were moving, I found out my tuition would be increased dramatically because I would be classified as a non-resident. I was paying my own tuition, so I had to follow my family to Texas. After moving to Texas, I changed colleges three times in search of a great art department. Finally, I gave in and decided to just get my degree. I am sure going to college in New York would have changed my style.

My quilts are an expression of my art. I could do art in any medium, but I'm closer to the textiles. I've done it for so many years, I feel confident I can express almost anything that I want to express in fabric.

WREN IN THE BIRDHOUSE, 2007 ● 7 x 10 inches (17.8 x 25.4 cm) ● Silk crepe; inkjet printed, hand painted, free-motion embroidered ●
Photo by Rick Wells

How I Work

My current series is called *City Birds*. I live in the Kingwood section of Houston, Texas, and I travel to different, interesting parts of the city to take photos. Then I connect a digital projector to my computer and view the images. I choose the best ones and start visually composing. Then I sketch, sketch, and re-sketch.

Once I have the composition, I draw it full size or enlarge it on the printer. I always hang it up on the wall, leave, and come in later, trying to view it fresh. If something doesn't feel right, I leave it up until I can figure it out. Then I decide what techniques will best

convey the message of the work. For the *City* pieces, I chose shades of black, gold or silver, and blue. I wanted the starkness that buildings have. Clean lines and minimal colors. When I do woods scenes, I love the greens and browns, then surprises of colors—like finding a bloom on the path as you walk through the woods.

My techniques vary, depending on the best way to convey the image and message. I can include hand painting, silk-screening, airbrushing, and inkjet printing. I also use machine embroidery. I love this technique for its freedom of movement and the rich

CARMINE TRIO, 2007 ● 20 x 29 inches (50.8 x 73.7 cm) ● Silks, cotton; dyed, painted, silk-screened, machine embroidered, machine quilted ● Photo by artist

texture it adds. It is stunning when combined with appliqué. I combine it with beading by machine, fused patchwork, and special effects with tulle. Each technique has its own nuances. For instance, with silk-screening I can repeat imagery, but with airbrushing I get a soft layer of paint.

Telling Stories

I find nature so fascinating. Through my artwork and quilting, I try to tell stories of nature. I did a series on the yellow warbler. The cowbird lays its egg in the warbler's nest. The cowbird egg is blue and the warbler's eggs are white with brown speckles, but the warbler parents do not recognize that it's not their own egg. The cowbird nestling is this big ugly brown baby.

It knocks the baby warblers out of the nest, and the warblers end up raising it. The cowbird ends up being about twice as big as the warbler parents while it's still a fledgling in the nest.

The editor of my book *Quilted Sea Tapestries* had an author party and she invited me back to her house in Seattle, Washington. She had a salmon run behind her house, which I had never seen. They actually put a ladder in the stream to help the salmon go back up the stream to spawn and lay their eggs. She told me about salmon, and then I researched them. They are an amazing fish, because they start out in fresh water, live most of their lives in salt water, then go back to fresh water to spawn and die. My research led to a large triptych depicting the salmon's life cycle.

CARMINE COLONY III, 2009 ● 32 x 42 inches (81.3 x 106.7 cm) ● Silks; dyed, silk-screened, painted, machine embroidered, machine quilted ● Photo by Rick Wells

City Birds

I feel birds mimic their surroundings. I love their songs and sounds, the combination of their movements. When I studied endangered birds, I was amazed at how much land each pair of birds needs. Yet, in the city, birds flock together, flying in formation, and take over entire intersections. I love their nests, which can be in signs, on light posts, or in drainpipes. Birds are very resourceful.

I hope that viewers will look at the world with fresh eyes because of what I've created.

birds

SUE KONGS ● ON GOLDEN POND, 2010 ● 33½ x 34 inches (85.1 x 86.4 cm) ● 100% cotton and cotton batiks; hand and machine appliquéd, machine quilted ● Photo by Thomas Kongs

JOANNE BAETH ● SUNSET AND
SANDHILL CRANES, 2009 ●
53 x 48 inches (134.6 x 121.9 cm)
Cotton fabrics, hand-dyed fabrics, inks,
paints; raw-edge appliquéd, thread painted,
machine quilted ● Photo by Robert Jaffe

DIANE HAMBURG ●
BEACHCOMBERS, 2009 ●
21 x 27 x ½ inches
(53.3 x 68.6 x 1.3 cm) ●
100% cotton, vintage book pages,
beads, shells, driftwood; raw-
edge appliquéd, spray painted,
stenciled, machine quilted ●
Photo by artist

DONNA JUNE KATZ ● STARDUST, 2009 ● 32 x 35 inches (81.3 x 88.9 cm) ● Unbleached muslin, thinned acrylic paint, whole cloth; hand painted, hand quilted ● Photo by Tom Van Eynde

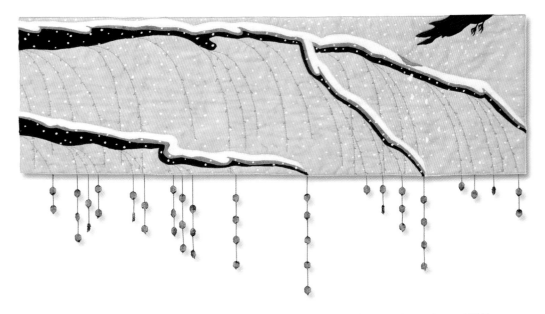

KAREN SCHULZ ● WINTER'S LEAVING, 2005 ● 19 x 34 inches (48.3 x 86.4 cm) ● 100% cotton, paint, vintage glass beads; fused, machine appliquéd and quilted, hand embroidered ● Photo by PRS Associates

LINDA FROST ● GOLDEN BIRD, 2006 ● 16 x 30 x ¼ inches (40.6 x 76.2 x 0.6 cm) ● 100% cotton hand-dyed and purchased fabric; machine thread-painted, machine quilted ● Photo by artist

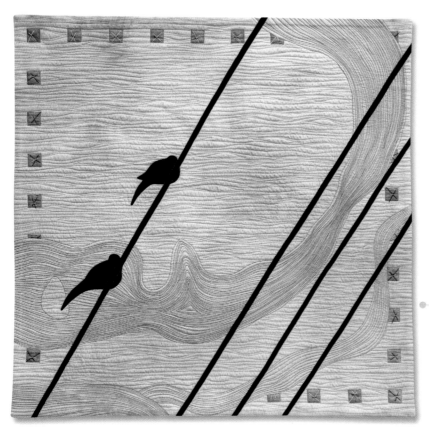

LESLIE A. HALL ● CONVERSATION AT DUSK, 2008 ● 30 x 30 inches (76.2 x 76.2 cm) ● Pima cotton; dyed, machine appliquéd, machine quilted, hand embroidered ● Photo by Philip W. Hall

MARGARET DUNSMORE ● THE LOON AND HIS MUSIC, 2005 ● 20 x 55 inches (50.8 x 139.7 cm) ● 100% cotton, hand-painted water fabric, rayon and cotton threads, fabric paint, stencil paint; hand appliquéd, machine pieced, raw-edge machine appliquéd, machine quilted Water fabric by Marianne Leeke ● Photo by artist

SHARON MCCARTNEY ● OLD IN STORY, 2010 ● 30 x 18½ x ½ inches (76.2 x 47 x 1.3 cm)
Vintage linens, linen, cotton, silk organza, acrylic paint, stones, wool, thread; hand and
machine pieced, hand quilted, embroidered ● Photo by John Polak Photography

SALLY DILLON

CAREFULLY OBSERVED AND DETAILED birds, fish, mammals, and crustaceans are combined in Sally Dillon's work with beautiful aerial views of the areas where they live. The soft sheen of her silks and the rich depth of her colors create a surface that draws the viewer in for closer inspection. A central panel, with either an aerial map or landscape overview of a particular location, is surrounded by carefully depicted vignettes showing different aspects of that particular environment: mother birds guard their babies; a cormorant dives for his dinner; waves swirl and eddy. In each place where the sashing that divides these miniature scenes intersects, there's another tiny inhabitant. Each piece is very site specific—these are the animals, rocks, and plants that can be seen at this location, though some might require a microscope. Together, they create a joyous celebration of the wonders of the natural world around us.

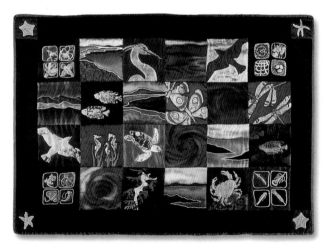

NATURE'S SAMPLER, 2005 ● 46 x 63 inches (116.8 x 160 cm) ● Silk; hand painted, hand quilted ● Photo by University of Massachusetts Photo Services

Science Background

Science was my main academic interest from grade school through high school, including wonderful summers as an intern at a National Science Foundation Laboratory in Connecticut. I decided to attend Mount Holyoke College to pursue a career in biochemistry, but during freshman year I took a course in art appreciation and was totally hooked. What could be better than making pictures and sculptures of the things I had seen in the lab?

Art Training

I continued my study of studio art at the University of New Mexico, making huge sculptures out of fiberglass, wood, and dyed fabric. Working on a tight budget, I bought or scrounged yards and yards of plain burlap and canvas and dyed them in trash cans over wood fires in the desert before sewing them into giant body parts and creatures. Unfortunately, one "masterpiece" was mistaken for trash by the university's clean-up crew!

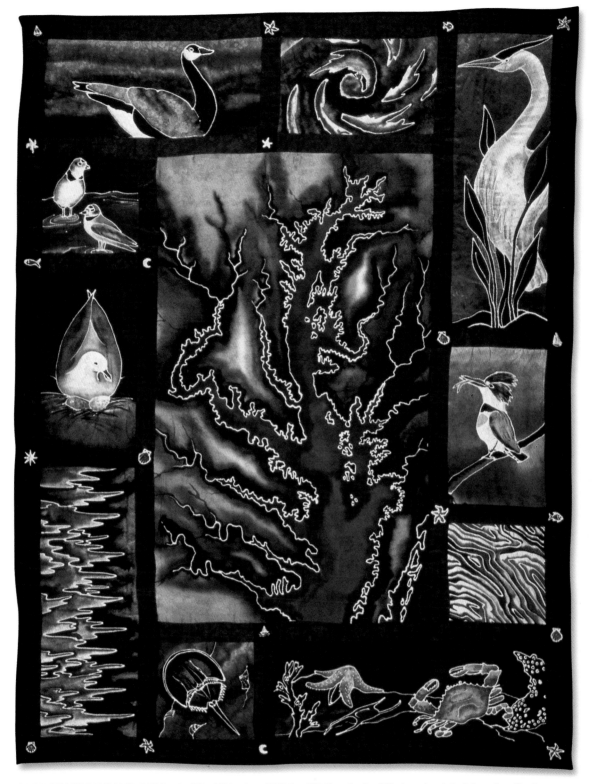

CHESAPEAKE BAY BLUE, 2005 ● 72 x 55 inches (182.9 x 139.7 cm) ● Silk; hand painted, hand quilted
Photo by University of Massachusetts Photo Services

ST. JOHN, V.I., 2000 ● 65 x 89 inches (165.1 x 226.1 cm) ● Silk; hand painted, hand quilted ● Photo by John Polak

From 1970 to 1988 I worked for a commercial art and design crew in Dallas, Texas, designing, building, and organizing all kinds of exhibitions, special events, and theatrical productions. These collaborative projects were great fun and provided me with lots of experience in welding, working with wood, and painting and dyeing fabric on a large scale. I also learned many important lessons about working with clients, working within a budget, and the challenges of site-specific projects.

Silk Painting

In the 1980s we adopted our two children, and I needed a more flexible schedule, so I decided to go into the art-making business for myself using my silk painting methods. Using the highest quality silk and colorfast dyes, I stretched the fabric over a frame and drew a line of wax resist before applying the dye with watercolor brushes. The works were then dried, steamed, washed, and dry-cleaned before being sewn into scarves, clothing, and wall hangings. Working with silk was and continues to be a pleasure. It's thin, soft, and pliable, yet strong, precious, and ancient. By using it to make art, I feel that I am taking part in a long tradition of wedding usefulness to beauty.

I kept up my interest in science and was inspired by a course I took in structural geology.

The Harvard Mineralogical Museum in Cambridge hosted my first silk painting show based in part on pieces in their collection.

An Aerial View

I enjoyed mixing strictly geological pictures with images from trips to the western national parks, and I did a series of scarves, jackets, and quilts based on the Grand Canyon, Arches, and Bryce Canyon National Parks. As I continued my series, I found that there was so much to show about each of these locations that I began to break up the picture plane into sections, so I could fit more information into each piece. I started using the center panel for a map or aerial view and the side panels for details and close-ups of the rocks or plants in the location. Aerial views reveal so much about the drainage, the fault line, and what is happening on the land that can't be seen from the ground.

Inspiration

In 1995 our family moved back to Amherst, Massachusetts, from Texas. I began making silk pieces incorporating seasonal color changes, inspired by the quilt-like farmland and the soft curves and ever-changing colors of the Holyoke Range. Although this "everyday" beauty inspires most of my work, I am still attracted to exotic landscapes and love to take trips that involve new visual experiences. Learning to scuba dive and snorkel has opened up a whole new world of imagery. We have been to Hawaii, Cozumel, and the Caribbean, and I never miss an opportunity to go to an aquarium. I enjoy fish and coral almost as much as rocks.

SEA LIFE, 2002 ● 50 x 59 inches (127 x 149.9 cm) ● Silk; hand painted, hand quilted ● Photo by University of Massachusetts Photo Services

WOODS HOLE, MA, 2002 ● 48 x 48 inches (121.9 x 121.9 cm) ● Silk; hand painted, hand quilted ● Photo by University of Massachusetts Photo Services

The *Woods Hole* quilt was a commissioned piece. The client is a scientist at the Woods Hole Marine Biological Laboratory and invited me to come and draw the creatures that they study there. They are famous for their work with horseshoe crabs, sea slugs, and long-finned squid. I sent sheaves of watercolor drawings to the scientists there to be vetted before I ever put a brush to silk.

Color

The actual color—or the "feel" of the color—of the subject and area inspires most of my silk paintings. But occasionally I start with a color group from nature (like the purples and gold of the fall) and try to make my subject conform to that color restriction. I particularly enjoyed making an all black-and-white swamp

piece called *Bayou Country* when the actual swamp I was working from was almost completely green. It was an interesting challenge, and I felt that I was able to show more subtle detail by having a limited color palette.

Working Methods

The *St. John* quilt was commissioned by a Massachusetts family who owned a house in the Virgin Islands. They asked to trade a two-week stay in their villa for a silk quilt that depicted the view from their house there. Before I went, I measured and photographed the space in their Massachusetts home where the finished quilt would hang. Arriving in St. John, I filled my sketchbook with large watercolors of birds, fish, sugar mills, termite nests, and fantastic views. I snorkeled every

BIG BEND NATIONAL PARK, TEXAS, 1993 ● 83 x 56 inches (210.8 x 142.2 cm) ● Silk; hand painted, hand quilted ● Photo by artist

DILLON BEACH, 2004 ● 55 x 42 inches (139.7 x 106.7 cm) ● Silk; hand painted, hand quilted ● Photo by John Polak

day and took pictures with an underwater camera to remind me of what I had seen. When I returned to my studio, I made a small painting of the whole quilt to scale, made full-size color drawings of each section, and silk painted color samples for their approval. I used that drawing as the pattern, pinning each finished silk painting on the paper original as it was completed. Working in this way gave me an opportunity to see the whole composition develop and make any necessary changes in color, scale, or detail. When all of the 11 main sections, 24 small corner pieces, 34 sashing pieces, and back pieces were painted, I did the piecing by machine. Then the hand quilting was skillfully done by my friend Janet Hale.

Nature

I've always been fascinated by the patterns and shapes of the natural world—the outline of a mountain range, the geometry on a turtle's back. When I studied geology and geography, I found beauty in maps, aerial photographs, and hydrological diagrams. It is exciting to continuously discover new designs in nature's infinite array of imagery.

● Sally Dillon

KAREN ILLMAN MILLER

MOST OF US DON'T GIVE MUCH THOUGHT to diatoms, a common type of algae found in damp environments. Karen Illman Miller has not only thought about them, she's made numerous works that celebrate the beauty of their naturally radial symmetry. Diatoms, trout, jellies, and octopi seem to float through water, while the denizens of the Northwest tide pools—starfish, sea stars, and anemones—also cavort across her works. Miller lovingly depicts the spiral shells of fossil ammonites, ancestors of both the modern chambered nautilus and of the octopus, and other naturally occurring plant and animal patterns. She uses a katazome stencil-dyeing process based on traditional Japanese techniques, laboriously carving many detailed versions of each plant or animal in different positions and sizes. Using either indigo vat dyes or washes of watercolor pigment mixed with soymilk, she dyes and paints her designs in nuanced, delicate colors. The cumulative effect of the intricate beauty to be seen in each portrayal of the natural world is simply astonishing.

MIZU MANDALA III, 2007 ● 41 x 41 inches (104.1 x 104.1 cm) ● 100% silk; Japanese stencil dyed (katazome), machine quilted ● Photo by Shadowsmith Photographics ● Collection of Dr. Jane Lubchenco

Why Quilting?

To be honest, my mother was a painter and a good one, and I needed to find a medium that did not feel like a competition I could never win. I resisted quilting for a long time because pieced quilts at that time seemed to lack spontaneity; once the pattern and fabric were chosen, all the decisions were made, and I lost interest. An early class with Nancy Crow convinced me that both piecing and quilting could be much freer. Quilted art made a much more dramatic presentation on the wall, and the tactile nature of fabric and thread just felt right. And I love the slight sculpted layer formed by the quilting. Once I added katazome stencil-dyeing to the mix, I was confident that I had found the creative voice we all strive for in our art.

Japanese Influences

My maternal grandfather was an early naturalist in the Pacific Northwest. He founded the University of Washington's marine lab in Puget Sound and traveled

GEOLOGICAL CLOCKS, 2002 ● 41 x 24 inches (104.1 x 61 cm) ● 100% silk; Japanese stencil dyed (katazome), stamped, machine quilted ● Photo by Shadowsmith Photographics

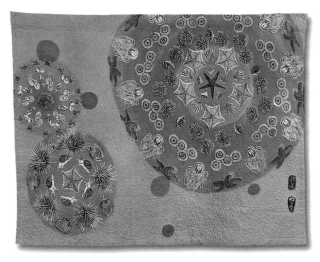

MIZU MANDALA I, 2002 ● 41 x 52 inches (104.1 x 132.1 cm) ● 100% silk; Japanese stencil dyed (katazome), machine quilted ● Photo by Shadowsmith Photographics

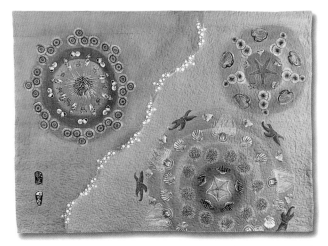

MIZU MANDALA II, 2003 ● 39 x 54 inches (99.1 x 137.2 cm) ● 100% silk; Japanese stencil dyed (katazome), machine quilted ● Photo by Shadowsmith Photographics

to Japan in 1912 at the request of the United States government. The house was full of art and artifacts from Japan. I love the asymmetrical composition of Japanese art, the subtlety and sometimes the audacity of the color combinations, and particularly the respect and imagination that the textile designers have for the native plants and animals of Japan.

Marine Biology

As I was growing up, my grandfather's basement workshop was filled with marvels such as insects in boxes and animals in glass jars. I fell in love with marine intertidal animals as a child and eventually earned a Ph.D. in zoology. I spent most of my career studying the structure and function of the intricate and beautiful blue blood proteins of *Octopus*. I realize only now that I was responding to this research topic at least as much as an artist as I was as a scientist. The radial symmetry of these animals was captivating my eye even as their structure and function were captivating my mind.

I design my own stencils using the plants and animals that have always inspired me. I am not as comfortable with abstraction or interpretation; I find real beauty in structure. It matters to me that a scientist would recognize one of my starfish or leaf skeletons as zoologically or botanically accurate. Lately, I have been concentrating on abstract patterns that appear in natural forms. I see the world of pattern with much the same delight as a taxonomist views sorting plants or animals into logical and related groups.

The Importance of Home

I have lived in Corvallis, Oregon, for 40 years. Everything grows lushly here, as the summers are warm and the winter climate is mild. The winter light is soft, and the colors are muted and tender. Nature has something to offer in all seasons. The cold waters of the Pacific Ocean support incredibly rich marine life. I am not sure I could live in a place without such diversity of plant and animal life. I could still do katazome anywhere, but I would have to look farther for my inspiration.

What Is Katazome?

Katazome is Japanese stencil dyeing. It starts with a hand-cut paper stencil. I use traditional Japanese stencil paper (shibugami) that's made from two or three

HEADING HOME, 2008 ● 23 x 43 inches (58.4 x 109.2 cm) ● Silk, cotton; Japanese stencil dyed (katazome), hand quilted ● Photo by Shadowsmith Photographics

layers of kozo (mulberry paper), laminated with fermented persimmon juice (kakishibu), and smoked. It is brittle when dry and allows me to cut extremely detailed patterns.

After it is cut, I attach a layer of silk mesh (sha), which holds all the delicate parts together. I soak it in water before I use it, and the paper becomes leathery and tough and clings to the fabric, so when I spread rice resist paste through it, I get very precise images. I steam the paste and add glycerine and calcium hydroxide to condition it. It looks like warm peanut butter, smells like brown rice, and dries down on the fabric very tightly—if you get it on the counter, you have to chisel it off. But after 20 minutes in warm water, it is gone. It holds up to indigo dyeing in a vat and can be painted with any thickened dye. I most often use powdered watercolor pigments mixed with fresh soymilk, because I can get extremely delicate color gradations.

The transparency of the colors allows a kind of iridescent layering that I find more beautiful than solid colors.

Working Process

I mostly work from photographs, but because I am designing stencils, the images have to be simplified. I edit as I cut to simplify a design, or I scan images into Photoshop so I can convert them to high-contrast black-and-white. Then, when the image gets painted, even if it goes back to the original colors, it is no longer photorealistic, but one step abstracted. Simple does not mean lacking in detail, however. The more intricate the image the more fascinating I find it. I compose as I lay the paste, without any planned design or layout.

I start by designing new stencils or selecting ones from among the hundreds I have cut over the past 15 years. I wash and pre-treat the fabric with soymilk to stiffen it and prepare it to receive the dyes. I apply the paste and

DIATOMS 2, 2009 ● 37 x 39 inches (94 x 99.1 cm) ● 100% silk; Japanese stencil dyed (katazome), machine quilted ● Photo by Shadowsmith Photographics ● Collection of Dr. Jane Lubchenco

then I either dye the whole thing and add detail colors, or paint the details first and protect these areas with more resist paste before dyeing the background. I can add more stenciled resist paste and repeat this process several times, building up successive layers of images to get the finished fabric panel. My trout and salmon quilts took most of a week to paint, because I had to wait for each layer to dry.

Whether I hand or machine quilt depends on the level of precision a particular piece requires. For delicate natural forms, hand quilting works best. If I want texture or thread painting effects, machine quilting is faster and easier.

Indigo Dyeing

Indigo dyeing involves taking insoluble blue indigo dye and rendering it soluble with alkali and then reducing it to remove the oxygen. The soluble indigo is a screaming yellow green, which turns blue before your very eyes when the fabric is exposed to air. It has never stopped being almost magical to me.

Indigo is perfect for katazome because it does not require a lengthy immersion to pick up color. I dip my indigos at least five times to build up the color, allowing the resist paste to dry completely between dips. It is a dye that attaches to the surface of the fabric, which means the resist paste protects the fabric completely down to the finest details.

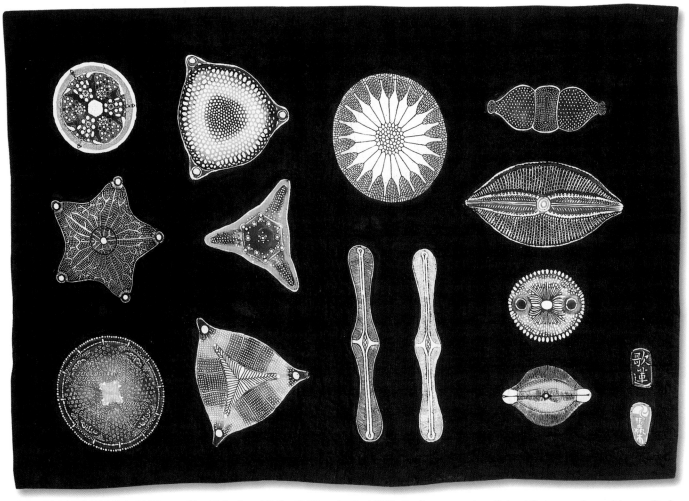

COLLECTOR'S ITEMS 2, 2003 ● 32 x 45 inches (81.3 x 114.3 cm) ● 100% silk; Japanese stencil dyed (katazome), machine quilted
● Photo by Shadowsmith Photographics

Color

I started working first with indigo, but my artist's eye prefers a variety of colors in my work, at least some of the time. I battle the temptation to be too literal with colors. However, the stencils are tools in which I have invested countless hours. I owe it to myself to use them many times, so I like to challenge myself to compose with them in stylized ways, in which case all rules are off with respect to color. For example, with the diatoms, I remember thinking that they are truly nature's jewels, like multicolored glass; hence I made them all different colors in *Collector's Items*.

Respect for the Natural World

I want to share with people the immense power of the katazome process for producing patterned fabrics with discrete imagery. I want them to remember the respect I feel for the natural world, the richest source of inspiration there is.

water

HOLLY ALTMAN ● TIDAL POOL—AFTER THE STORM, 2009 ●
40½ x 31 x 2 inches (102.9 x 78.7 x 5.1 cm) ● 100% cottons, poly-
esters, felt, tulle, paint, beads, water-soluble lace, yarns; machine
appliquéd, machine quilted ● Photo by Carolyn Wright

DIANE MARIE CHAUDIERE ● LOOKOUT,
2009 ● 39 x 14 x 1 inches (99.1 x 35.6 x 2.5 cm)
● Cotton and mixed fibers, beads, paint; hand
pieced and embroidered, machine quilted ●
Photo by artist

C.J. PRESSMA ● PRECIOUS OBJECTS, 2007
81⁹/₁₆ x 76 inches (207.2 x 193 cm) ● Cotton;
inkjet printed, machine quilted ● Photo by artist

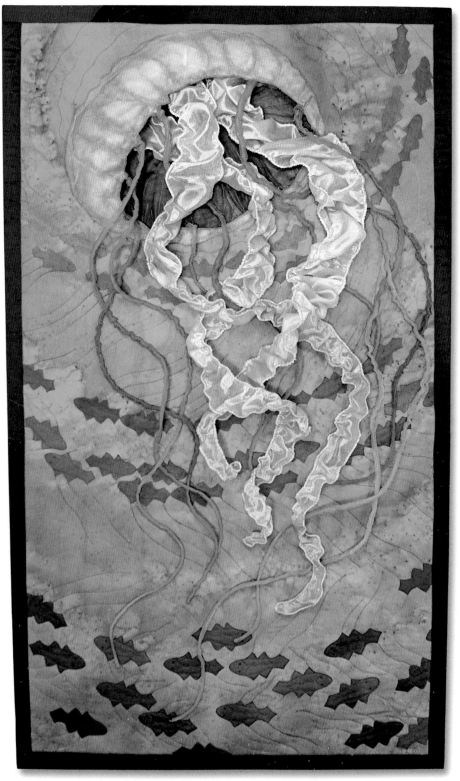

C. SUSAN FERRARO ● MOONDANCE, 2004 ● 69 x 40 x 7 inches
(175.3 x 101.6 x 17.8 cm) ● Hand-dyed cottons, silks, sheer voiles, electrolumi-
nescent lighting, cotton batting, seed beads; hand and machine pieced, hand and
machine quilted ● Photo by artist

ELLEN ANNE EDDY ● BALCONY SCENE, 2003 ● 36 x 30 inches (91.4 x 76.2 cm) ● Hand-dyed cotton, novelty brocade, rayon, hand-painted organza and cheesecloth, metallic and nylon threads; direct appliqué, machine-embroidered appliqué, machine embroidered and quilted ● Photo by artist

BETH MILLER ● TURRET CORAL, 2001 ● 39 x 47 inches (99.1 x 119.4 cm) ● Hand-painted and dyed cotton fabric, commercial cotton fabric; fused appliqué, machine quilted ● Photo by David Patterson

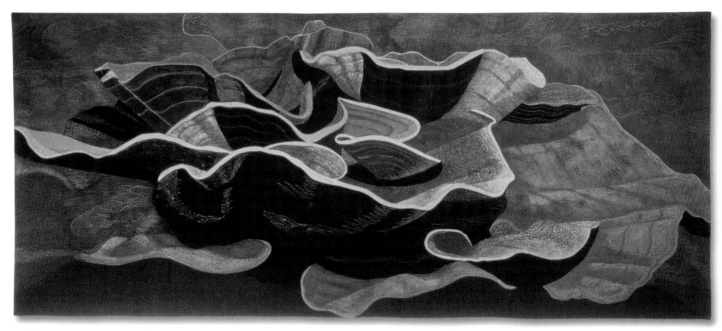

HOLLIS CHATELAIN ● CABBAGE CORAL, 1996 ● 20 x 48 inches (50.8 x 121.9 cm) ● 100% cotton fabric, cotton batting; hand dyed and painted, machine pieced and quilted ● Photo by Lynn Ruck Photography

HOLLIS CHATELAIN ● ELKHORN CORAL, 1998 ● 25 x 52 inches (63.5 x 132.1 cm) ● 100% cotton fabric, cotton batting; hand dyed and painted, machine pieced and quilted ● Photo by Lynn Ruck Photography

JAYNE BENTLEY GASKINS ● TORTOISE, 2009 ● 8 x 11 x 1½ inches (20.3 x 27.9 x 3.8 cm) ● Cotton broadcloth, inkjet inks, photograph printed on cloth, polyester batting; thread-painted, trapunto quilted ● Photo by artist

CASSANDRA WILLIAMS

IT'S BEEN SAID THAT THE EYES are the windows to the soul. The power of Cassandra Williams' animals is certainly their marvelously soulful eyes. Each animal is composed of hundreds of raw-edge appliquéd pieces placed against a simpler pieced background. The animals can be realistically colored or created with riffs of maroon, orange, and teal zebra stripes. Each creature seems to have a very distinct personality as it looks directly out at us with great emotion. The animals engage us with their direct gazes, yet they seem at peace. While much modern artwork depicting animals is designed to be consciousness-raising, demanding environmental action, these pieces are simply lovingly detailed portraits of each animal's serene beauty and stately grandeur.

BULL'S-EYE, 2005 ● 72 x 62 inches (182.9 x 157.5 cm) ●
100% cotton, inks, paints, machine-pieced grasses; raw-edge appliquéd, free-motion machine quilted ●
Photo by Al Williams

Twins

I was born a twin in Minneapolis, Minnesota. My sister Cynthia and I have competed in every way since birth. We share a very close bond, and we believe that we truly are one person divided in half. When she started oil painting, I naturally followed suit. For most of my life I was an oil painter, specializing in nudes and old buildings. I've lived in about half of the United States, and I dragged those framed paintings all over the country.

When I retired, I wanted something different, something fresh yet creative and easy to store. I started quilting and competing in quilt shows, and, of course, Cynthia became my competitor. Sometimes she is the winner, sometimes I am, but it never really matters because we're doing something together. Since she lives near Atlanta and I'm in Oregon, we don't see enough of each other.

The idea of going back to my previous themes and quilting a nude has intrigued me over the years, but, to be honest, since my pieces nearly all go into international competition, I've been hesitant to provoke any judges.

JIGSAW GIANTS, 2002 ● 74 x 50 inches (188 x 127 cm) ● 100% cotton, tulle; machine pieced, raw-edge appliquéd, free-motion machine quilted ● Photo by Al Williams

RIVER RUN, 2002 ● 37 x 69 inches (94 x 175.3 cm) ● 100% cotton, tulle, paint; machine pieced, raw-edge appliquéd, free-motion machine quilted ● Photo by Al Williams

SONORA DESERT BLOOMS, 2004 ● 77 x 61 inches (195.6 x 151.9 cm) ● 100% cotton, tulle, paint, inks; machine pieced, raw-edge appliquéd, free-motion machine quilted ● Photo by Al Williams

I may do one for my home yet. When I started making quilts, old buildings took a backseat to animals. My first art quilt, a cougar, was so pleasing to me that one critter just led on to the next. Several animals are currently on my to-do list, starting with a close-up of a huge turtle.

Pacific Northwest

My husband (of over 50 years) and I are retired in Grants Pass, Oregon. Many years in the South and in the western deserts sent us seeking a green, wet place. The wildlife of the Pacific Northwest has definitely inspired my interest in portraying animals. Our yard is overrun with deer and wild turkey. Bear, cougar, and fox visit regularly. Some of my work might have happened if I lived somewhere else, but not the Lewis and Clark quilt (*The Map Makers*, owned by the National Quilt Museum in Paducah, Kentucky), the cougar, or river fish quilts. They are pure Oregon.

My Husband's Photographs

My husband and I owned a skin-diving business for several years and dove in many warm-water locations. We taught diving, waterskiing, and surfing. I've seen small octopus while we were diving in the Bahamas, Hawaii, and Mexico, but unfortunately none as big or colorful as mine in *Dance of the Deep*. I drew him from my imagination.

My husband, Al, is quite a photographer, and I often use his photos for inspiration. I also have a friend who has gone on several safaris and has sent numerous pictures to me for my research. The giraffes and zebras are based on those photos.

Since my animals need to be anatomically correct, I do research online and in libraries, but I always draw my own designs. Other than research on the Internet, I don't use the computer. As an artist, I want to create the work from my own imagination and use my drawing talent.

I think each animal draws me into its own world. I like to get up close and personal with each one. The colors and textures fascinate me. That bull may look brown from a distance, but to me its coat shades from ecru to charcoal, with every shade of taupe and rust in between. I want to make that work through the use of commercially printed and sometimes quirky fabrics. My landscapes are memories of places we have lived and are my "photo albums."

Process

Once an idea is formed in my head, I research the anatomy of each animal carefully and then proceed with several preliminary sketches. From a small line drawing—about 10 x12 inches (25.4 x 30.5 cm)—complete with shadowing and highlights, I create a full-sized version that is the size of the finished quilt. This becomes my pattern. I draw in the shapes of the details on the paper pattern, usually several hundred of them, and then I trace them all onto a full-sized sheet of muslin. The muslin is hung on my design wall and becomes the base onto which I pin a collage of fabrics following the pattern.

I use tracing paper to copy the pieces from the master pattern in order to cut out my fabrics. When the pieces pinned to the muslin seem to be just right, I remove each pin and lightly glue-baste each piece, with just enough glue to hold until it's quilted. When the art piece is completed, I add batting and backing and proceed to the free-motion quilting. Each piece, no matter how small, must be stitched around at least once. A very narrow binding is my favorite; I almost never use a border because I don't want to frame the scene but prefer the work to just stretch out forever in the viewer's mind.

HERE KITTY, KITTY, 2001 ● 37 x 41 inches (94 x 104.1 cm) ● 100% cotton, tulle; raw-edge appliquéd, free-motion machine quilted ● Photo by Al Williams

Universal Appeal

Trying to please not only myself but also traditional quilters led me to include geometric blocks in many of my backgrounds. I wanted to reach as many viewers as possible with my work and found that it worked for me as well. My background choices are often determined by the habitat of the subject as well as the all-important light and shadow balance necessary in the piece. It's the animal that calls me; his habitat is important, but secondary in my mind.

Color Choices

Until recently, my color choices have been fairly realistic. I might add a yellow sky, lavender-blue water, or a purple-skinned walrus to provide enough color variety to satisfy me. However, lately I've been influenced by my wilder quilt friends to branch out into some more unusual color choices. I'll never be into modern art, but I am learning to fly with brilliant color.

I use a few hand-dyed fabrics, and occasionally I need to paint a human's face and hands. I build my palette of

WALRUS ON THE ROCKS, 2003 ● 33 x 42 inches (83.8 x 106.7 cm) ● 100% cotton, paint; raw-edge appliquéd, free-motion machine quilted ● Photo by Al Williams

commercial fabrics during my travels: I buy a half-yard of any "nature" fabric that catches my eye. For example, I must have 200 greens in my stash, but since I don't use much of any one piece, that will probably last me a lifetime. I never go out shopping for specific fabrics when designing a quilt. That would be much too distracting. Once the blown-up version of the design is ready, I can't go shopping!

Feelings of Tranquility

When a viewer first sees one of my quilts, I hope she says, "Wow, look at that!" Then I want her to get a warm feeling that she will take home in her mind, even if she forgets the subject of the piece. For instance, my giraffes have such a look of softness in their eyes that many people have felt the tranquility pouring out from that quilt. This is what I'd like viewers to remember about my work.

DANCE OF THE DEEP, 2003 ● 53 x 68 inches (134.6 x 172.7 cm) ● 100% cotton, tulle, beading, paint; embroidered, embellished, raw-edge appliquéd, free-motion machine quilted ● Photo by Al Williams

BETTY BUSBY

PAY CAREFUL ATTENTION—THERE ARE DANGERS lurking in the depths of the natural worlds celebrated in Betty Busby's work. Even long-dead raptors may suddenly awake to take a bite out of their portraits. Busby's strong desire for clean lines and uncluttered design leads to crisp, careful edges, but the crocodiles, eels, and carnivorous dinosaurs she depicts seem likely to erupt into a more natural chaos at any moment. Eschewing fur-covered mammals, Busby focuses instead on invertebrates, fish, birds, reptiles, and amphibians. She finds their bodies more interesting and their lives more beautiful. Continual experiments with materials and techniques are part of Busby's struggle to find the most effective way to communicate her passion for these often-ignored species of the animal kingdom.

TEMPTATION REEF, 2010 ● 40 x 42 inches (101.6 x 106.7 cm) ● Over-painted cotton batiks, velvet, silk organza, dupioni, cotton, cheesecloth, produce bags, pearls, dryer sheets; turned-edge machine appliqué, burned, hand beaded, machine quilted ● Photo by Allen Mitchell

Influence of Place

I was born in Sasebo, Japan, in a military family. Although we moved from there when I was young, the Japanese aesthetic has had a very profound influence on me. Jun Kaneko from Nagoya was my professor and my degree project advisor during my senior year at the Rhode Island School of Design. His philosophy of putting art first in your life stays with me to this day.

I've lived in Albuquerque, New Mexico, since 1994. The clear beauty of the high desert has definitely found its way into my work. It has a starkness that I resisted until fairly recently but appreciate now. Even though I continue to portray many kinds of natural scenes in my work, from the ocean to the jungle and forest, I believe that my environment has influenced me to portray them all fairly cleanly, without extraneous clutter. If I lived somewhere else, I don't think this would be happening.

Ceramics and Fiber

My background in ceramics has had a profound effect on the fiber work I produce today. I enjoy semi-controlled experiments and love the surprise results. Running a manufacturing company I founded, Busby Gilbert Tile, Inc., for nearly 20 years taught me a lot about working hard and gave me the ability to find numerous and creative ways to get things done.

WELCOME TO THE JUNGLE, 2010 ● 68 x 54 inches (172.7 x 137.2 cm) ● Silk dupioni, silk habotai, artist-dyed cottons, nonwoven materials, lace, beads; turned-edge machine appliqué, fused, couched, machine quilted ● Photo by Allen Mitchell

ANNIE'S CROW, 2009 ● 40 x 18 inches (101.6 x 45.7 cm) ●
Silk dupioni, silk habotai, batiks, nonwoven materials; turned-
edge machine appliqué, fused, thread-painted ● Photo by
Allen Mitchell

While majoring in ceramics in college, I also took
fiber design classes. It was a great alternative to
ceramics—light, colorful, and non-dusty! I have been
making quilts since the 1970s. When I lived in Venice,
California, I began dyeing old curtains and picking
clothes out of trash cans to sew. I approach fiber art
with the same values as I approached ceramics. I enjoy
finding new products to use and inventing new techniques to highlight them. I also work at it every day as
a business. Besides creating the pieces, they must be
catalogued, entered into shows, and marketed.

Fiber is intrinsically beautiful, but I am drawn to it
for several additional reasons. The uncontrollable surprise factor of dyeing and painting it in experimental
ways directly recalls my nearly 20 years as a ceramicist,
when each kiln firing produced different effects in the
glazing. Fiber can also be manipulated in infinite ways
with sewing techniques, which add to the depth and
interest of the final work.

Inspiration

I work from my own snapshots. The dinosaur bones,
for example, came from dozens of pictures I took at the
Natural History Museum in Philadelphia. The quality of the picture isn't important, because I never use
the photos exactly as they are. I draw my work out freehand, using the photos simply as references.

I'm also inspired by images I find on the Internet. I
check the APOD (Astronomy Picture of the Day) web-
site every day. It is a NASA site that posts a new picture
of the skies every day. I have also become addicted to
the Nikon Small World and Olympus Bioscapes micro-
photography sites: there are amazing things we can't
see with the naked eye!

Computer Use

The computer is an invaluable help to me at many
stages of the design process. Frequently, a large piece
of hand-painted and/or dyed fabric is the jumping-
off point for the entire piece. I'll photograph it on
the design wall and then print it out in color on plain
paper. This allows me to sketch all over it with colored pencils, and if the design isn't working, it's easy to
print out another and start again. This method makes
it easy to come up with dramatic compositions, and,
since the printout is the same scale as the background

URCHIN, 2010 ● 27½ x 30½ inches (69.9 x 77.5 cm) ● Hand-woven over-painted silk, nonwoven material, cording; fused, couched, machine quilted ● Photo by artist

fabric, I can get a general idea of the size of the elements to be made without wasting a lot of time on trial and error.

The computer can also enlarge my scanned sketches to the needed dimensions, which reduces a lot of redrawing time. Partly completed projects are photographed and loaded into the computer. Then it's easy to do the time-tested artist checks of reversing or inverting the image, or changing the image to black and white in order to check the balance of the composition.

Color and Technique

I love variety and will often follow a vibrant piece with a more subdued one.

The choice of the background material is frequently the basis of the color scheme. Even though most of it may not show in the finished work, it still gives me a base to "bounce" other colors and textures off of. This gives a harmonious color flow throughout the piece.

Much of my work is technique-driven. I enjoy discovering new abilities to construct an image in different ways. I never set out to make something "pretty." The appearance of each project is determined by the idea behind it. Creating my own raw materials is also important, and I have been dyeing my own fabric since I began quilting over 30 years ago. I am interested in and familiar with fabric construction from the raw fiber on up.

Temptation Reef

Each work is different and a new form of experimentation. However, all of my works are linked by the fact that each aspect of a piece is evaluated and re-evaluated during every phase of its construction.

As an example, I was inspired to create *Temptation Reef* by a group of Elaine Quehl's hand-dyed fabrics, which she gave me as a gift. Elaine takes many types of material—silk, velvet, cotton, and cheesecloth—and immerses them in the same dyebath. She sells them as "Temptation Packs." The one she gave me was pistachio

STYRACOSAURUS, 2009 ● 64 x 56 inches
(162.6 x 142.2 cm) ● Cotton sateen; dyed/discharged,
resist painted, machine quilted ● Photo by Allen Mitchell

HENRY THE OCTOPUS, 2009 ● 36 x 40½ inches
(91.4 x 102.9 cm) ● Artist over-painted batiks, nonwoven
materials; machine quilted, painted, turned-edge machine
appliqué, fused ● Photo by artist

green, and I challenged myself to make something that would use all of the materials in a cohesive manner.

First, I chose a patterned dark batik and over-painted it with dark purple on the bottom and iridescent white at the top to give the illusion of depth. Then I air-brushed patterns on some of the fabric and used paint sticks on others. Several large elements were then fused to the over-painted background and quilted. I painted over some of the quilting, and appliquéd and couched additional design elements over the ones already in place. The entire piece was then quilted again, hand beaded, and bound. Forming the composition over many steps allowed for changes to be made during each step of the process.

The Animals

I frequently portray reptiles, fish, amphibians, and insects because their bodies are not obscured by a covering of cute, fluffy fur. The inner workings of their bodies are explained by their outward appearance, and I find their alien yet familiar qualities endlessly inspiring. Truthfully, it's never occurred to me that these subjects could be scary or repellent!

I have loved dinosaurs since I was three years old, and as an alternate career I would have been a paleontologist. To see these bones, millions of years old, stripped of their flesh, is an intensely moving experience for me.

Art and Making Things

I believe that making art is a vital part of what it is to be a human being. Extensive teaching experience has shown me how important learning basic drawing skills and art appreciation is even to the youngest children.

My entire life has been spent making things. To me, each piece is about communication. I want to tell a story or express an idea or an emotion. I judge the success of each piece by the effectiveness with which it communicates its message.

I'd like to be able to communicate my love of my subject matter, from slimy snails to scary raptor skulls, and to share a bit of the joy I feel in being privileged enough to work at art full time.

MAGPIES, 2009 ● 53 x 39 inches (134.6 x 99.1 cm) ● Polyester, silk habotai, nonwoven materials, batiks; turned-edge machine appliqué, fused, thread painted ● Photo by Allen Mitchell

ANNIE HELMERICKS-LOUDER

WHEN A COW IS STANDING ON A TABLE and blue herons are strolling through a living room, you take notice. Annie Helmericks-Louder's animals turn up in the most unusual situations as part of her bid to make us sit up and pay attention to how we regard and treat the animals around us. A formally trained painter, Helmericks-Louder works in many different media, including oils, pastels, and charcoal, as well as cloth. The common thread running through all of her artwork is a celebration of the beauty found in the natural world. Colors and compositions are often surreal, because she is not trying to mirror reality but to chronicle her response to it. Her vignettes may be unlikely, but the juxtaposition of animals and their surroundings invites us to create stories to explain their actions and interactions. Helmericks-Louder hopes that through our shared stories we can create a connection with each other and with the other beings with which we share the planet.

OUTLAW ANIMAL: JACKRABBIT, 2010 ● 77 x 72 x 2½ inches (195.6 x 182.9 x 6.4 cm) ● Manipulated and dyed commercial fabrics, hand-woven cloth, hand-dyed silks; raw-edge appliquéd, reverse appliquéd, crocheted fabrics, hand embroidered, hand and machine stitched, hand quilted ● Photo by Gregory Case

Not a Fiber Artist

I do not think of myself as a "fiber artist." I think of myself as a person who makes things. When I am traveling and away from my studio, I most often work *en plein air* (outdoors), creating pastel drawings or acrylic paintings. Each medium, however, has its own essence. For example, the scratch and gesture of charcoal is often the perfect choice for capturing a rough desert landscape, while the sheen and slickness of charmeuse silk may speak wonderfully about the shine of a long-still pond.

I must confess that I truly *love* cloth, yarns, threads, and all things textile. Laying out a palette in oil paint, for example, is a necessary preparation for the work to follow. Sifting through cloth however, feels like the work itself: The fabric seems to tell me what the work will become. Paint and pastel on their own do not usually inspire a piece of work, but when I see a stack of cloth—well, that is another thing.

SIDE BY SIDE: THE DINNER GUEST, 2001 ● 95 x 79 x ½ inches (241.3 x 200.7 x 1.3 cm) ● Metal milagros, manipulated commercial cottons, hand-dyed silks; block printed, drawn and painted with dyes, turned-edge appliquéd, hand and machine stitched, hand quilted ● Photo by Bryan Tebbenkamp

NO PLACE AT THE TABLE, 2010 ● 83 x 82 x ½ inches
(210.8 x 208.3 x 1.3 cm) ● Manipulated commercial cottons,
hand-dyed silks; raw-edge appliquéd, hand embroidered, hand
and machine stitched, hand quilted ● Photo by Gregory Case

Importance of Place

I was born in Montrose, Colorado, and raised mostly in
southern Arizona. I currently live on ten acres of wooded
land in rural Missouri. Where I live always affects my
work. I am an autobiographical storyteller, and all my work
begins with an experience, memory, or dream. I prefer to
linger, dance, and play in wild places and to fill my heart
and eyes with this planet's indescribable beauty. I am
haunted by it.

Message about the Environment

We have become the deadliest species on this planet. Our
behavior toward other species—and the planet itself—
indicates an almost total disregard for the sacredness,
interconnectivity, and value of life. I'm not suggesting
that we should not take part in the cycle of living as witnessed by the life stages of all plants and animals, as life
lives from other life. But we demonstrate unforgivable
irreverence and irresponsibility. For example, the commercial, inhumane warehousing of our slaughter species
(agricultural animals) denies all value of them as living
creatures. It is ironic that "humane," the very word we use

for kind treatment, has "human" as its base. Where is the
word that includes the other species? For most of my artistic life I have chosen to turn away—go to pristine places to
paint. But this is becoming harder and harder as we use up,
defile, and impoverish the planet.

Working Methods

Inspired by experiences in New Mexico and Arizona,
Outlaw Animal: Jackrabbit is the second work in my ongo-
ing *Outlaw Animals* series. This series features "vermin"
animals, those designated as having no value.

During the summer of 2010, I made over 40 *en plein air*, full-
sheet pastel drawings. This direct, on-the-land experience
left me with a hypersensitive awareness of intricate natural
textures and patterning. During the same travels, I acquired
several boxes of beautiful vintage and designer cloth.

The hardest part about using beautiful cloth is to find
ways to make it your own, and I wondered how I could pos-
sibly cut into these treasures. After admiring it for a few
days, I started to dramatically alter some of the yardage

through distressing and deconstructing it—over-dyeing, combining, slicing, unraveling, and re-weaving and re-assembling the cloth.

At the same time, I pinned up some of my drawings for design and color inspiration. The sketch I selected for the background was from an actual experience with a jack-rabbit, so I was able to use my own photographs for this "story." However, my pictures showed the rabbit mostly running and leaping, so I also used other images from the Internet to clarify "my" rabbit. I used Photoshop for the final design process. I printed out a to-scale pattern, which was taped together from letter-sized pieces of paper. It was used for the shape of the large sections rather than for detailed images.

I had to assemble the work in sections due to its scale, so I divided the image into foreground, middle ground, and background pieces. As I wanted to focus on texture first, I began with the foreground—physically working to collage, integrate, and attach these heavy fabrics. These elements were pinned and then hand and machine sewn onto a sturdy cloth support.

The background was constructed next, with middle ground following, and all the sections were sewn together. The rabbit was the final element added. I hand-quilted all the layers together with heavy mercerized cotton thread using a stippling stitch. The way I quilt leaves a long floating stitch on the back of the quilt and clearly evidences the presence of my hand in the stitching.

Unusual Colors and Perspectives

Many feel my perspectives and combinations of imagery and colors are unusual. As a formally trained academic artist and teacher (I teach design, painting, and drawing), I recognize "realistic" perspectives and color. As an artist and human being, however, my work represents how the world appears to *me*. Gravity, so to speak, does not apply in my works. I do not feel that my role as an artist is to record. It is, instead, to interoperate.

My use of color is a little harder to explain. I have done an *en plein air* painting, certain I am painting what I see, only to go home and find that while my photographs indicate I was in a green forest, my painting shows all the foliage clearly red! All I can say is that the forest, right then, *felt* red. I use color as a way to express experience and emotion. These choices are visceral.

SIDE BY SIDE: BLUE HERONS, 2001 ● 72 x 80 x ½ inches (182.9 x 203.2 x 1.3 cm) ● Manipulated commercial cottons, hand-dyed silks; block printed, painted, discharged, turned-edge appliquéd, reverse appliquéd, hand stitched, hand quilted ● Photo by John Louder

THE TRINITY TREE, 2009 ● 59 x 54 x 1 inches (149.9 x 137.2 x 2.5 cm) ● Manipulated commercial cottons, hand-dyed silks; raw-edge appliquéd, hand embroidered, hand crocheted, hand and machine stitched, hand quilted ● Photo by Bryan Tebbenkamp

BIG FISH, 2008 ● 82 x 57 x ½ inches (208.3 x 144.8 x 1.3 cm) ● Manipulated commercial cottons, hand-dyed silks; raw-edge appliquéd, hand embroidered, hand and machine stitched, hand quilted ● Photo by Bryan Tebbenkamp

SLEEPING WITH THE COWS, 2008 ● 79 x 57 x 1 inches (200.7 x 149.9 x 2.5 cm) ● Manipulated commercial cottons, hand-dyed silks; raw-edge appliquéd, hand and machine stitched, hand quilted ● Photo by Bryan Tebbenkamp

Importance of Writing

Reading influences my work—especially reading writers who use beautiful visual words. I come from a family of writers and we read out loud together. Although the poetry that frequently appears in my artist's statements is my own, I don't consider myself to really be a poet or writer in the true sense of the word. But poetry, like art, allows ideas to be explored in a non-linear way. The cadence of poetry and the beauty of certain phrases often accompany me in my mind as I make images. I have come to realize that many viewers find they help them to decode my images, so I sometimes include them for that reason.

Encouraging Awareness

My new grandson will probably never see a wild polar bear or a free jungle parrot. Will there be any left? It would appear we are, perhaps, running out of time. My work

questions established hierarchies, and I hope it encourages sentience and awareness.

However, the strong, underlying message in my work is simpler: It is my human experience. My life is not unusual. Like others, it is filled with pedestrian experiences, ordinary passages of life and time. But I propose that every ordinary life is extraordinary; daily life is amazing! Friendship, a beautiful day with fall colors, the miracle of a birth, the worries of our children, and the grief and loss from a death—we all experience these things. Through my work I seek to establish and reconcile my own understanding. My visual stories are just sketches, though, and, read as linear narratives, they are narrow and small. It is my hope that what I can create instead are frames for stories that include enough specificity and enough openness to touch people in their lives. I hope that they can find and make their *own* stories within them.

OUTLAW ANIMAL: SKUNK, 2011 ● 90 x 64 x 2 inches (228.6 x 162.6 x 5.1 cm) ● Manipulated and dyed commercial fabrics, hand-dyed silks; raw-edge appliquéd, hand embroidered, hand and machine stitched, hand quilted ● Photo by Gregory Case

animals

MICHELLE JACKSON ● THE BLACK-TIE AFFAIR, 2010 ● 43 x 41 inches (109.2 x 104.1 cm) ●
100% cotton fabrics, laces, organza, fur, velvet, yarn; fused appliqué, machine quilted ● Photo
by Nathan Jackson

NANCY S. BROWN ●
GIRAFFES, 1997 ●
50 x 70 inches (127 x 177.8 cm)
● 100% cotton; hand appliquéd,
machine pieced, hand quilted ●
Photo by artist

TANYA BROWN ● SIESTA, 2010
33 x 45 inches (83.8 x 114.3 cm)
● Whole cloth, 100% cotton, ink;
thread painted ● Photo by artist

LESLIE GABRIËLSE ● SAFARI, 2004
70⅞ x 47¼ inches (180 x 120 cm) ●
Fabric, acrylic paint; hand sewn ●
Photo by artist

CAROL TAMASIUNAS ●
HOT SPOT, 2010 ● 20 x 24 x ¼
inches (50.8 x 61 x 0.6 cm) ● 100%
cotton, paint; hand embroidered,
machine quilted ● Photo by artist

MICHELLE JACKSON ● BUCKY, 2010 ● 43 x 47½ inches (109.2 x 120.7 cm) ● 100% cotton fabrics; fused appliqué, machine quilted ●
Photo by Nathan Jackson

NANCY S. BROWN ● GORILLA GORILLA, 2007 ● 47 x 56 inches (119.4 x 142.2 cm) ● 100% cotton; hand appliquéd, machine pieced, hand quilted ● Photo by artist

RUTH POWERS ● LONGHORN
SPLASHDOWN, 2010 ●
33½ x 47½ x ¼ inches
(85.1 x 120.7 x 0.6 cm) ●
100% cotton commercial prints;
machine pieced, free-motion
machine quilted ●
Photo by artist

NANCY ERICKSON ●
EASTER COUGAR, 2001 ●
46 x 72 inches (116.8 x 182.9 cm)
● Velvet, satins, cottons,
whole cloth, fabric paints,
oil sticks; quilted, machine
stitched, and appliquéd ●
Photo by artist ● Collection
of the Holter Museum of Art,
Helena, Montana

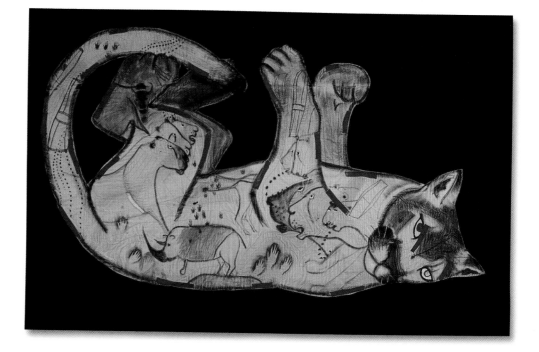

DOMINIE NASH

JOHNNY MERCER'S SONG "AUTUMN LEAVES" CONJURES up a poignant image of passing time and regret. Dominie Nash explores actual fallen leaves in her work, memorializing them in rubbings of stark black and white or warm shades of brown. The neutral colors of her compositions focus our attention on each leaf's distinctive shape, with its branching stems and intricate veining. The leaves she collects are used either in their entirety or in a skeletonized state. Hand stitching adds emphasis to each leaf's structure, while layers of organza overlays partially obscure and shift what is visible. Part of what attracts Nash to the leaves is their impermanence. The leaves that she works with are exactly how she discovers them. Using what nature provides creates design spontaneity that is an important component of her process. The leaf images often seem to fade into the background, reminding us of the inevitable passage of time and the cycles of the seasons.

BIG LEAF 10, 2007 ● 42 x 42 x ¼ inches (106.7 x 106.7 x 0.6 cm) ● Cotton, silk, organza, textile paint; machine appliquéd and quilted ● Photo by Mark Gulezian/Quicksilver

Beginnings

My background is in the social sciences, and I have a master's degree in social work. After I discovered that social work was not for me, I went to graduate school but didn't like the field I had chosen. I'd always sewn my own clothes and knitted, so I decided I would try to pursue some of those interests. I'd met a few people who were doing fiber art of various kinds, which was a revelation to me. I got a loom and I wove for many years. While I was weaving, I saw the landmark (traditional) quilt show that started at the Whitney Museum of American Art and I was just blown away by the color and the whole visual impact of the quilts. But when I experimented with making functional quilts for my family, I became frustrated trying to make a perfectly pieced quilt. I pretty quickly decided that I just had to make quilting my own, so I started breaking some of the rules, started making my designs a little off-kilter.

I have since been asked "Why fiber?" many times, and sometimes in a critical way, since my work seems far from its traditional roots. My answer is that the work would not be the same if it were not in fiber; there are qualities inherent in art made of fabric and thread— the particular depth of the colors, the layers, and the texture of the stitches—that can't be duplicated in another medium. Handling and placing the fabrics to create a composition is a totally different process than

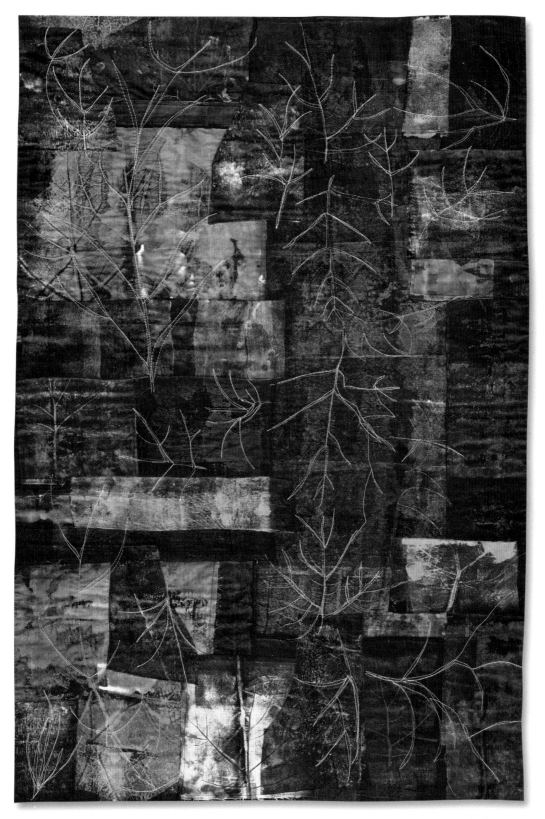

BIG LEAF 17, 2008 ● 52 x 34 x ¼ inches (132.1 x 86.4 x 0.6 cm) ● Cotton, silk, organza; discharge paste, machine appliquéd and quilted ● Photo by Mark Gulezian/Quicksilver

BIG LEAF 22, 2009 ● 59 x 29 x ¼ inches (149.9 x 73.7 x 0.6 cm)
● Cotton, silk, organza, dye, textile paint; machine appliquéd
and quilted ● Photo by Mark Gulezian/Quicksilver

working with brush and canvas or paper. I don't wish to emulate or compete with painting but rather to make good quilts that reflect these special characteristics. I have recently tried some printmaking, which I love, but I can't imagine not doing it on fabric and adding stitches.

Techniques

I pretty much dye or print everything I use in my quilts. Any way I can get pigment or dye on fabric I've experimented with. I use a variety of surface design processes, including immersion dyeing, painting with dyes and pigments, screen-printing, monoprinting, Inko-printing, chemical resist, and discharge. The surfaces are layered with dyed organza, which can enhance or change the color beneath it, and finished with machine stitching and embroidery.

Big Leaf Series

I have long been fascinated with the shape and structure of leaves of all kinds. A few years ago I came across some very large leaves. I printed fabric with them, and this was the start of a new series. The resulting quilts are mostly whole cloth, with the leaves taking center stage, enhanced by accidental patterns created by the printing tools, variable amounts of paint, etc. The large hand stitching echoes the vein patterns of the leaves.

I start by deciding which leaves to use or by looking through my already-printed fabrics. Sometimes I have some new leaves and am eager to use them, so that determines the design. I then print several pieces of fabric, using either a frottage rubbing technique with textile paint or deconstructed screen-printing with thickened dye. I pin up fabrics that I think will work well together; when I am satisfied with the arrangement, I baste and machine-stitch down the individual pieces, essentially raw-edge appliquéing them onto the batting and backing. The stitching is done through all layers, not just the quilt top. The next step is to add organza overlays, pinning, rearranging, and finally stitching them down with a very fine thread. Other than occasional hand embroidery, quilting is the next and final step before I finish the edges.

My entire working process is as spontaneous as I can make it, but the final stitching is probably the most spontaneous thing. I just sit down at the sewing machine and start quilting, and the thread just sort of meanders, and I never know exactly what it's going to look like. Sometimes I have to rip out a lot of the machine quilting because it just doesn't work.

Collage Process

Whether a particular piece is representational or abstract in nature, I work in a collage-like manner. The layers that result from the overlapping of forms, lines,

and fabrics are of particular concern to me, creating a sense of mystery and depth. I hope that the viewer will see more and different things at each viewing. The coloring and patterning of the fabric are essential elements in my attempt to achieve this goal; the uneven and serendipitous results contribute to the spontaneity and expressiveness of the work, even though the composition may be planned in advance.

Color

For the leaf pieces, I try to stick to black and white or neutrals, as the shape and structure of the leaves is

BIG LEAF 23, 2009 ● 49 x 65 x ¼ inches (124.5 x 165.1 x 0.6 cm) ● Cotton, silk, organza, dye, textile paint; machine appliquéd and quilted ● Photo by Mark Gulezian/Quicksilver

BIG LEAF 5, 2006 ● 72 x 20½ x ¼ inches
(182.9 x 52.1 x 0.6 cm) ● Cotton, silk,
organza; discharge paste, machine appliquéd, hand quilted ● Photo by Mark
Gulezian/Quicksilver

more important to the design than their colors. With works in my other series, I think the palette is intuitive or emotional—I often have no idea what the colors will be until the initial design on paper is done, and I take out my colored pencils and start scribbling. I then make a lot of color changes when I start to work with the fabrics. Occasionally, I use the actual colors in the objects I portray but less so recently. I am more interested in abstraction and in expressing a mood or feeling than in rendering an object realistically.

Working in a Series

I like to work in series because it's a way to develop my ideas and have a body of work that hangs together. I never think that I'm going to do 10 in a row or four or whatever—it just happens. At some point with most series, I know that I'm finished exploring that idea, but with other series I come back to the idea again and again. I usually have two or three different series that I'm working on at the same time, which may not look anything like each other. So I have to be careful when I'm presenting my work so as not to confuse people. I usually pick one series or another to show someone who is interested in my work. I think consistency is important to people.

I guess it all stems from the fact that I get very uncomfortable when I have a blank piece of paper in front of me. Over the years, I've found that I was just frustrating myself by trying to draw out what I wanted to do. Starting with directly placing the fabrics on my design wall is much more freeing than drawing. I'll just start cutting shapes, and then all of a sudden I will see something is happening, and I can go on and add to it and complete the composition. Sometimes I'll just pin up some big hunks of fabric that I like on the wall and start putting other things on top. I overlap things, and I leave the edges raw, so that I can change anything as I go along, and I really like that.

Spontaneity

Friends and family find big leaves for me; this adds an element of collaboration, and I enjoy the spontaneity of working with whatever comes along. Using actual leaves makes the work easier, as my printed fabric provides the first layer of the design—I never know exactly what the fabric will look like until it's finished, and I love leaving it to chance.

BIG LEAF 18, 2009 ● 37 x 19½ x ¼ inches (94 x 49.6 x 0.6 cm) ● Cotton, silk, organza, dye, textile paint; machine appliquéd and quilted ● Photo by Mark Gulezian/Quicksilver

KATHERINE K. ALLEN

A LYRICAL USE OF NATURAL MATERIALS, particularly grasses, weds Katherine K. Allen to the places where she lives. Her technique requires her to think and work in a way that many would consider backward. First, Allen chooses the colors for the details of a composition and paints or stains the entire whole-cloth piece in that palette. Then she creates a stencil using actual grasses and other items. Finally, she paints in the background using an overprinting technique. When she removes the grasses, their silhouettes are preserved in the original colors, and details can be added with paint or stitch. This complex technique has become so natural to Allen that her process is filled with quick, intuitive gestures. She rarely changes or edits the compositions. Her aim is simply to capture the essence of the natural world that surrounds her.

ALMOST ALONE, 2010 ● 53 x 60 inches (134.6 x 152.4 cm) ● Cotton, acrylic paint, screen-print inks; two layers, machine stitched ● Photo by Gerhard Heidersberger

The Importance of Place

My work is reflective of where I am and what I am experiencing. I grow or gather all of the plant materials used in making my artwork, which means I spend a great deal of time outside. Weather, light, and surrounding scenery profoundly influence the palette and mood of my compositions. I have lived for almost 30 years in Florida and for the past several years have also maintained a studio in Maryland on the Eastern Shore of the Chesapeake Bay.

The starkly differentiated lights and darks of South Florida present a world of shape, shadow, and silhouette that is abstracted in my work. Tropical sunlight influences the saturation of many of my color choices. In Maryland my studio is located in a wood at the edge of a creek. My work there tends to be more grayed and less chromatically intense but equally graphic.

Natural Materials

I cultivate lemongrass, switchgrass, sedges, cattails, ferns, and other plants specifically for my artwork. I prefer fresh specimens, but pressed leaves work, as do string, paper, plastic sheeting, and quilt batting. I find that working with live plant material weds me to season and location and by extension keeps the

FEASTING ON STARS, 2009   ●   Each panel: 67 x 20 inches (170.2 x 50.8 cm)   ●   Silk, acrylic paint, screen-print inks, batting; hand and machine stitched   ●   Photo by Gerhard Heidersberger   ●   Collection of Christy and Sandy Price, Oklahoma City, Oklahoma

TANGLE, 2008 ● 21 x 42 inches (53.3 x 106.7 cm) ● Silk, acrylic paint, screen-print inks, batting; machine stitched ● Photo by Gerhard Heidersberger

EVENTIDE, 2009 ● Each panel: 53 x 36 inches (134.6 x 91.4 cm) ● Silk, acrylic paint, screen-print inks; hand stitched ● Photo by Gerhard Heidersberger

QUIET TALK, 2010 ● 25 x 53 inches (63.5 x 134.6 cm) ● Silk, acrylic paint, screen-print inks, batting; machine stitched ● Photo by Gerhard Heidersberger

work authentic. Whatever I am making is of a specific moment and reflects the qualities and realities of that time, place, and state of mind.

An important philosophy of cooperation and harmony with nature is implicit in my technique. By conflating the gestures and marks of nature with those of the human body, I am making a statement about their inextricability. We are one with nature, not separate from it.

Technique

Visualizing the experience I want to reference—its composition, visual flow, and emotional content—is the first step in creating a new work. I decide on color next and mix all the pigments I will use in the painting and printing steps. I get out my books on calligraphy, Japanese painted screens, and Abstract Expressionism, all of which are conscious influences on my work. By doing this, I am recalling the economical way in which a fluid mark contains and expresses energy and meaning. Also, I am reminded of particular compositions I find pleasing. I turn on music by Mozart and begin to color my cloth.

I apply an overall diluted color with acrylic pigments. Texture and line are added by squirt, spray, splatter, fling, and wipe. At this stage, I am painting the character but not the specifics of my subject. Fluid marks and washes reflect the organic nature of my botanicals. The initial placement of these hues, values, and textures will later be apparent, though much is obscured during the printing phase to come.

Paint dries as I gather stenciling materials from my garden or from the wetlands where I cultivate plants especially for this purpose. I work quickly in order to capture the freshness of my subject. I arrange my plant materials, string, and other small items intuitively atop the painted fabric. I am now ready to print.

The printing is not technically complicated, but it is messy and requires strength. I squeegee screen-print inks through a completely open silk-screen. I then lift the screen and shift it laterally, repositioning it to overlap coverage areas slightly, and pull the ink again. Progressing in this manner, I ink the entire surface of the cloth. When the composition is dry, I may turn the inked leaves over and use them as stamps. Or more stencil materials may be added and another color applied. The final color is the lightest value and visually describes the character of the space around the plant forms.

Stitching

Stitching is the last step in the process and requires a bit of rumination. I incorporate both hand and machine stitching in response to the rhythms and character of the design. I think of these stitches as textural and atmospheric as well as structural. They animate the surface and provide an enriching textural experience when the artwork is viewed up close. I choose silk fabric for most of my work because of the way it takes pigments and because it can more easily be stitched by hand. Hand stitches invest my art with touch, time, and intimacy. On cotton fabric I use free-motion machine stitching. With both techniques I keep the stitching expressive and reminiscent of a drawn line or mark.

Design Process

I never design my work on paper or computer. Spontaneity is a quality I strive to preserve in my work. Above all, I try to keep it fresh. I think of myself as "drawing" with the plants and grasses I use in my designs. The process is somewhat unpredictable, and I never know exactly how the inks will react to my stencil materials. I try to observe, recall, and concentrate as I create and let the images emerge organically throughout the process of covering and revealing. I use my cameras a great deal. I am always on the hunt for interesting silhouettes of plants and unusual birds.

My birds are captured on camera first and then drawn and painted by hand. The birds are added to my designs in one of three ways: at the beginning, using hand-cut stencils; printed directly, using a silk-screen; or painted on by hand.

SUMMER LUXURY, 2010 ● 52 x 104 inches (132.1 x 264.2 cm) ● Cotton, acrylic paint, screen-print inks; hand stitched ● Photo by Gerhard Heidersberger

SONG TWICE OVER, 2010 ● 52 x 60 inches (132.1 x 152.4 cm)
● Silk, acrylic paint, screen-print inks; machine stitched ●
Photo by Gerhard Heidersberger ● Collection of Erika Kao,
Rancho Santa Fe, California

INTERWEAVE, 2010 ● 33 x 41 inches (83.8 x 104.1 cm) ●
Silk, acrylic paint, screen-print inks, batting; hand and machine
stitched ● Photo by Gerhard Heidersberger

Capturing the Essence

I am constantly learning more about color and trying
out new combinations of hues and degrees of inten-
sity. For the most part, my color choices are expressive
and responsive, rather than naturalistic or representational. I am influenced by Japanese painted screens,
Abstract Expressionism, and sumi-e. I refer to art
books on these subjects frequently to remind myself of
what I am trying to accomplish and how to most suc-
cinctly and powerfully animate my pictorial space.

I am drawn to the flattened, stacked compositions of
Japanese painted screens with their generous use of
potent, quiet spaces. Abstract Expressionism encourages me to use unexpected color and open-ended
description of form. Sumi-e, an extremely stylized
painting discipline, teaches me to focus my mind and
let my body lay down a mark with an informed, deci-
sive, fluid gesture. This way of working leaves a trace of
the particular moment of making. I am living this Zen
practice when I make marks and form shapes with my
scattered botanicals. I create using quick, intuitive gestures, rarely editing or rearranging.

A Sense of Community

I was trained as a sculptor. I first began exploring
fabric, paint, and stitch as a relief from the hard metal
and concrete of my sculpture. In the late 1990s I took a
class at a local quilt shop and learned to make a nine-
patch bed quilt. I learned to sew clothing as a teenager
in Oklahoma and fondly remembered the neighbor-
hood sewing group I belonged to there. Perusing books
on the history of quilting, I was particularly drawn to
whole-cloth narrative quilts. When I came across the
contemporary artwork of Nancy Crow and realized the
amazing variety and quality of what was going on in
the world of art quilts, I felt I had found my place. Here
was an art form that honored craft, showcased the elements of art, could be representational or not, told a
story, or simply dazzled the eye. The real kicker was
that, for the most part, it was created by women. An
immediate love of the materials and the sense of community I found in the world of fiber took hold of my
heart, and I have never looked back.

INTERLUDE, 2008 ● 42 x 33 inches (106.7 x 83.8 cm) ● Silk, acrylic paint, screen-print inks; hand and machine stitched ● Photo by Gerhard Heidersberger

leaves

MARY ARNOLD ● FALL'S FIRE, 2009 ● 40 x 41 inches 101.6 x 104.1 cm) ● Hand-dyed and batik fabrics; machine pieced, hand appliquéd, machine quilted ● Photo by Mark Frey

DIANNE FIRTH ● ONION, 2006 ● 51³⁄₁₆ x 51³⁄₁₆ inches (130 x 130 cm) ● 100% cotton; torn-strip machine appliquéd, machine quilted ● Photo by Andrew Sikorski

PEG KEENEY ● WILLOW, 2007 ● 58 x 52 inches (147.3 x 132.1 cm) ● Whole-cloth, sticks, silk, cotton, rayon, metallic threads; free-motion quilted ● Photo by artist

ANNETTE KENNEDY ● AGAVE CACTUS, 2009
● 22⅝ x 17¾ x ¼ inches (57.5 x 45.1 x 0.6 cm)
100% cotton; fused appliqué, painted, machine
quilted ● Photo by artist

CATHARINA BREEDYK LAW ● SAVIN' EARTH, 2010
● 65 x 42½ inches (165.1 x 108 cm) ● Cotton,
hand-dyed silks, rayon and cotton threads, paint;
machine pieced, free-motion quilted and embroidered, stenciled ● Photo by artist

ROXANE LESSA ● AMAZONIA, 2007 ●
48 x 35 inches (121.9 x 88.9 cm) ● 100% cotton,
polyester sheers, glass beads, paint; fused,
machine quilted ● Photo by artist

KATHLEEN LICHTENDAHL ● CLOSE-UP PRAYER,
2009 ● 19½ x 12 inches (49.5 x 30.5 cm) ● 100%
cotton treated with soy protein, watercolor pigments;
painted, machine quilted ● Photo by artist

SALLY SCOTT ● AXIS MUNDI REFLECTED, 2009 ●
92½ x 27⅛ inches (235 x 68.9 cm) ● 100% cotton,
hand-dyed string; machine appliquéd, machine
quilted ● Photo by artist

ANNEMIEKE MEIN

KNOWN FOR HER REALISTIC PORTRAITS of Australian animals, birds, and insects, Annemieke Mein bases her artwork on careful scientific observation, detailed sketches, and painstakingly drafted patterns. Each of her works is meticulously crafted and combines a wide range of textiles as well as a large array of different fiber techniques. While the background landscapes are often simply implied by a wash of watercolor or a few embroidered lines, the featured animals are minutely detailed and often partially three-dimensional, bursting out from the canvas. Mein's portraits are never static: baby birds quiver, frogs thrash in a whirlpool, and moths struggle to emerge from their cocoons. Nature's life forms are constantly growing, changing, mating, and dying. Capturing the essential energy of an incredibly wide range of creatures—even many that are often considered repellent, such as flies and barnacles—Mein shows us the infinite variety and inherent beauty of all of nature's creations.

DE LAPJES, 1991 ● 24 x 11 x 7 inches (61 x 27.9 x 17.8 cm) ● Dyed wool and mohair, crystal organza, dyed silk organza, satin, felt, covered wire, beads, polyester filler, machine threads, embroidery cotton; machine and hand embroidered, collage of wool and mohair under organza, padded, quilted, stuffed, pleated, shaped, beaded, dyed, plied, wired, lined ● Photo by Michael Page

My Background

I was born in Holland, but we moved to Australia when I was seven. Growing up surrounded by bush, where we lived in an outer suburb of Melbourne, has greatly influenced my work. Without many neighbors close by, I grew up living with nature and experiencing its beauty (and ugliness) daily. My fascination with wildlife developed into a passion for portraying it and sharing my experiences. Since I was isolated from the mainstream art world, I was free to develop my own style and methods.

Why Insects?

I have a special love and affinity for insects. I enjoy showing others the beauty of these tiny creatures through my works. I portray them larger than life using a myriad of textures and techniques to display metallic bodies; glistening, sheer, see-through wings; sparkling faceted eyes; as well as hairy legs, razor-like pincers, or twitching antennae.

DAMSELFLIES, 1995 ● 63 x 46 x 2 inches (160 x 116.8 x 5.1 cm) ● 100% cotton canvas, textile paints, embroidery threads, painted silk and crystal organza, commercially dyed silk organza, synthetic metallic fabrics, netting, felt, woven silk, iron-on interfacing, polyester filler, dyed pipe cleaners, recycled laminating plastic; painted, machine and hand embroidered, appliquéd, quilted, fabric collage, trapunto, plied, wired ● Photo by Michael Page

I believe that I cannot artistically or accurately portray an insect without first understanding it and its life cycle—eggs, larval stage, and adult—together with its proper care and nurture requirements. I need to understand an insect's eating habits, movement abilities, air and water needs in flight and swimming, mating and breeding methods, as well as its ecological impact.

For example, to create *Invasion*, I collected fly eggs and buried them in warm, moist compost in covered aquariums. The eggs hatched into larva (maggots) in 24 hours. The larvae were fed protein-rich fluids from composting meat. After five to six days of eating and growing, they dropped down into the soil layer and pupated. Adult flies emerged after five to eight days. Then they in turn mated and the life cycle was repeated several times each season. I studied them at each stage, watching, sketching, and making notes. Only after this type of intense study of the living creatures did I feel ready to start making my artwork.

The Importance of Sketching

I have always preferred to sketch my subjects. Sketches are able to capture an idea, a mood, an emotion, or an impression quickly. They can show a fleeting movement, as well as tonal values and textures, in just a few pencil strokes. My artwork developed in the era before digital photography and quick photographs were just not available.

But even with the advent of digital photography, I believe that one has to sketch mayflies "dancing" to achieve the motion and flow within the design. A photograph would only capture a static moment. Similarly, you need to witness a frog struggling to tread water in a whirlpool to sketch and sew it with true empathy for its efforts.

Using Fantasy Colors

My work may look realistic to the viewer, but that is really just an optical illusion. I could never recreate something as beautiful as what nature does so effortlessly. I just put together the colors, textures, and shapes that mimic our perceptions of insects, birds, fish, frogs, etc. For example, with a furry piece of fabric, I may be halfway to establishing a butterfly body. Then glittery glass beads and metallic threads convey the image of butterfly eyes, while khaki-colored wool fabric with appliquéd silk patches reflect insect-eaten eucalyptus leaves. Often a piece of fabric

FREEDOM, 1986 ● 39 x 55 x 4 inches (99.1 x 139.7 x 10.2 cm) ● 100% cotton canvas, textile paints, embroidery threads, painted silk organza, fur fabric, synthetic suede, silk, cotton, polyester filler, dyed and plied wool, embroidery threads; painted, machine and hand embroidered, appliquéd, quilted, collage, plied, trapunto ● Photo by artist

or fiber will inspire an idea, rather than the more usual sequence of the fabric being chosen to suit the subject. Some of my work uses very unrealistic, fantastical colors when I want do a work just for fun, for visual joy, for a laugh, or for a bit of drama.

My Creative Process

I make all of my textile works following the same sequence of steps. My daily walks around our home provide me with inspiration. I admire all types of Australian flora, fauna, and landscape. My observations and field studies are augmented by specimen collecting, breeding, and microscope observations. I am also fortunate to have been given loans of specimens by museums and collectors, and I own an extensive library of books that I use for reference.

I make dozens of preliminary sketches—small, rough, quick lines of the main subject—to capture the essence of what I want to portray, not just the actual animal or plant but also a feeling, a mood, or an idea. I try out mini-designs, small sketches of the main subject and background setting to get a sound integration of both.

Then I'm ready to create the full-scale design and layout plan. I draw everything using pencil on paper in full detail. This becomes the master design for pattern drafting, showing foreground, middle ground, and background open-space areas. I create a color scheme plan as well, in watercolor paint washes, colored pencils, or pastels.

The next step is to select my materials and fibers, ones that suit the texture, color, and mood of the main design. I may paint or dye my own fabrics or choose commercially available fabrics. I draft patterns from the full-scale layout, creating 30 to 500 pattern pieces, all numbered. I add seam allowances for the three-dimensional shapes if I am planning darts, pleats, quilting, sculpting, etc. This always reminds me of making a giant jigsaw puzzle.

Finally, I begin sewing, about 80 percent on the sewing machine and about 20 percent hand stitching, embroidery, and quilting. The percentages depend on how low- or high-relief the subject is designed to be: high-relief pieces require much more handwork. At each step of the process, I keep careful records of the work: daily notes and samples, trial-and-error records, costs and accounts in time and money, and photographs of each stage.

FACE ON, 1992 ● 65 x 44 x 3 inches (165.1 x 111.8 x 7.6 cm) ● 100% cotton canvas, textile paints and dyes, cotton, silk, synthetic and metallic embroidery thread, homespun and dyed silk fibers, commercial silks, combed wool, silk and crystal organza, metallic fibers, embroidered cotton, silk, and wool fabric, glass beads, dyed rabbit fur, felt, millinery wire, polyester filler, interfacing, woven wool, raw silk, gabardine, cotton canvas, imitation suede, silk organza, threads; hand and machine embroidered, appliquéd, collage of silk and wool under organza, drawn, painted, dyed, bound, plied, wired, felted, padded, quilted, stuffed, molded, layered, beaded ● Photo by Michael Page

My Fiber Art

My textile artwork is the culmination of many years of exploration of a multitude of fine arts and crafts. I have studied drawing, painting, sculpting (wax, wood, clay, and fiber), etching, printing, embroidery, patchwork, quilting, weaving, collage, and dressmaking. Each work today employs a diverse variety of combinations of technique. For example in *Invasion*, I used screen-printing, drawing, painting, quilting, fiber sculpting, embroidery (hand and machine), collage, and appliqué. In another piece, I combined drawing, painting, dyeing, binding, plying, wiring, felting, padding, quilting, stuffing, molding, sculpting, layering, and beading.

I just love the visual and tactile qualities of fiber. Since the 1970s, I have felt that I can express my love for nature and the environment better in textile works than in any other medium. I have been told many times that my work is a unique marriage of art and science. I hope that through my eyes and portraits, viewers will appreciate and nurture the natural world more closely.

HUNGRY MOUTHS, 1994 ● 33 x 28 inches (83.8 x 71.1 cm) 100% cotton canvas, textile paints, embroidery threads, silk organza, interfacing, polyester filler; painted, machine and hand embroidered, appliquéd, quilted, padded, plied ● Photo by Michael Page

WHIRLPOOL FROG, 1994 ● 41 x 67 x 2 inches (104.1 x 170.2 x 5.1 cm) ● 100% cotton canvas, textile paints, embroidery threads, painted silk organza, silk fabric, cotton, polyester filler; painted, quilted, stuffed, appliquéd, trapunto ● Photo by Michael Page

INVASION, 1996 ● 49 x 46 x 2 inches (124.5 x 116.8 x 5.1 cm) ● 100% cotton canvas, textile paints, embroidery threads, calico, polyester filler, silk organza; screen-printed, painted, machine embroidered, hand quilted, appliquéd, hand embroidered ● Photo by Michael Page

MELANI KANE BREWER

CHILDREN LOVE TO COLLECT CATERPILLARS and let them tickle their palms. Melani Kane Brewer is someone who has never outgrown her fascination with these small members of the animal kingdom. Captivated also by the beauty of the Florida birds, trees, and flowers that surround her, she is inspired to create wall hangings and framed vignettes that capture the intricacies of their lives. After careful study and documentation, Brewer uses thread painting to show the color and placement of each bird's feathers and the scales on each butterfly's wing. The thread-painted subject is then crafted into a three-dimensional body and placed in an environment with wonderfully textured leaves, grasses, and branches, which make the images come to life: tree trunks look rough, leaves seem as if they will start rustling, and feathery moth antennae gently wave in the breeze.

ESPERANZA~HOPE FOR THE TAMARINS, 2009 ●
21½ x 20½ x 1 inches (54.6 x 52.1 x 2.5 cm) ●
Hand-dyed 100% cottons, silk ribbon, exotic yarns, buckram, cotton batting, quilting and embroidery thread, hand-dyed cotton thread; drawing, thread painted, fused, tack stitched, machine quilted ● Photo by Gerhard Heidersberger

Florida Influences

Living in South Florida, with its wonderful climate, I am able to research and study year round. There are seasonal visitors, especially birds, so the view changes constantly. The state is full of wonderful creatures.

I'm not sure I would be creating fiber art at all if I had not come to Florida. My mother-in-law asked me to take a quilting class with her in an adult education program. When we started, and I saw those tiny quilting needles, I didn't think I could ever do it. I always used large needles and hated wearing a thimble, but I was up for the challenge and was soon making quilts. If my mother-in-law had not asked me to take that quilting class, I would never have started quilting on my own.

Three-dimensional Fiber

My mother worked in marble, clay, and porcelain, and I always marveled at her because thinking three-dimensionally seemed so foreign to me. As an art major in high school, I worked in clay, plaster, pen and ink, paint, scratchboard, and silver. Let's just say that my painting far surpassed my sculpting ability. I've never had the ability to start with a hunk of rock, take pieces away, and create something.

HERCULES MOTH, 2009 ● Each section: 4 x 6 x 1 inches (10.2 x 15.2 x 2.5 cm) ● 100% cottons, buckram, cotton batting, hand-dyed cotton thread, fabric markers, exotic yarns, reclaimed lobster-trap wood frames; drawing, painting, thread painted, fused, hand stitched, machine quilted ● Photo by Gerhard Heidersberger

WALK IN THE WOODS I~CECROPIA, 2005 ● 24 x 37½ inches (61 x 95.3 cm) ● 100% cottons, hand-dyed cotton, batiks, buckram, cotton batting, exotic yarns, quilting and embroidery thread, hand-dyed cotton thread, fabric markers; drawing, painted, thread painted, fused, hand stitched, machine quilted ● Photo by Gerhard Heidersberger ● Collection of Judy Black and Richard Schlosberg, Florida

AFRICAN STILT BEETLE, 2004 ● 12½ x 12½ x 1 inches (31.8 x 31.8 x 2.5 cm) ● Hand-dyed cotton fabric, exotic yarns, leather, cotton batting, thread; drawing, hand stitched, hand couched, machine quilted ● Photo by Gerhard Heidersberger

My mother also made beautiful gowns, suits, and hats by combining commercial patterns or designing her own. I was always around in her sewing room, watching, and I loved the feel and texture of the fabrics. Best of all, I got to play with the scraps. I should have known then that I would be a fiber artist.

Fiber and thread allow me to work three-dimensionally, building layers to create trees, birds, and insects. Strange as it may seem, I see the finished piece in my mind's eye before I ever start creating it.

Why Insects?

Insects are amazing and have been around for 435 million years. Many, like the praying mantis and the bee, are important ecologically. Although some might argue about mosquitoes, all insects have their place in the natural world.

My fascination with insects began the summer before the tenth grade. One of my summer projects was to collect insects for biology. Our family had a lake, where we would water-ski. It was surrounded by fields so I was in heaven: grasshoppers, crickets, butterflies, bees, dragonflies, stink bugs, and beetles were everywhere. My dad's garden was filled with every kind of insect you could imagine. My mother gave up her butler's pantry to pinning boards, jars, insect pins, cotton balls, and chloroform.

I haven't given up collecting. If I find any caterpillars, they come home with me along with their food-source plant. I place them in jars and wait for them to spin cocoons and hatch, and I release them into my garden after I photograph and study them. I also have plants that attract butterflies, so I can study all the stages of their life cycle. Zebra longwings, various swallowtails, skippers, and fritillaries are just some of the butterflies that visit.

Nestor, a Little Green Heron

Nestor really is a little green heron that visits the lake in my backyard. He also visits my neighbor's pool to eat the frogs. I started taking photographs of Nestor while he was hunting, or while he waited patiently on a tree branch that hangs low over the water.

I drew him on paper using the photos as a reference. I cut out the drawing and traced the basic outline onto buckram, then painted it with markers to match the colors of the bird, adding a few more lines for detail.

CATERPILLAR COCOON BUTTERFLY, 2003 ● 12 x 11¾ x ¾ inches (30.5 x 29.9 x 1.9 cm) ● Hand-dyed 100% cottons, exotic yarns, cotton batting, buckram, quilting thread, hand-dyed cotton thread; fused, hand and machine stitched, thread painted, machine quilted ● Photo by Gerhard Heidersberger ● Collection of Sarah Sterling, Cooper City, Florida

GUESS WHO'S COMING TO DINNER, 2004 ● 12½ x 12½ x ¾ inches (31.8 x 31.8 x 1.9 cm) ● Hand-dyed 100% cotton fabric, exotic yarns, thread, buckram, cotton batting; drawing, fused, hand stitched, machine quilted ● Photo by Gerhard Heidersberger ● Collection of Sarah Sterling, Cooper City, Florida

I thread-painted the entire body, changing thread as the colors of the feathers changed, which was often.

The wing was drawn on a separate piece of buckram and was stitched to the body at the top, while the bottom of the wing was left free to move. The legs are also separate; I thread-painted them last. Then I cut Nestor away from the buckram.

With the hard part over, I chose fabrics for the background. The base fabric was torn to the size of the finished piece. Since I don't bind my pieces, I left the edges ragged. To create the swampy look of the water, I tore pieces of fabric into narrow strips, leaving the edges raw.

Next, I started laying down pieces of exotic yarns. The colors and textures give depth to the water as well as dimensional depth to the piece from foreground to background. Grasses and reeds are made by fusing two pieces of fabric and then cutting them freehand.

The cypress trees were cut in sections and shifted around until I had them where I wanted them. Occasionally I set Nestor on the piece to see how he looked against the background. Layers of yarn and lines of stitching created depth in the cypress trunk. The cypress knees were layering with batting; each one was stitched in a freeform circular pattern and then attached to the background.

The branch that Nestor is standing on is three-dimensional and wired, so I could bend it as I wanted. The branch is about an inch (2.5 cm) away from the background surface. (Nestor's feet were hand stitched to the branch later.) Shaggy back feathers, ruffled by the wind, were cut from fused fabric and stitched in place at one end in multiple layers.

Frames

Framing pieces started as a way to increase sales. Visiting galleries and art exhibits, I noticed that all the pieces were framed. The first piece I framed was *Morning Mist*, and it sold on the opening night of the exhibit.

At a craft show, I met a couple that creates frames from reclaimed lobster traps. I loved the worn, rustic wood and purchased a few. Some of my insect pieces worked with the frames, and again they all sold. Although most of my works are wall hangings, I am always looking for interesting frames to use in my work.

SCHAUS SWALLOWTAIL BUTTERFLY, 2009 ● 4 x 6 x 1½ inches (10.2 x 15.2 x 3.8 cm) ● Hand-dyed 100% cotton fabrics, raw silk-wrapped paper, hand-dyed cotton thread, fabric markers, buckram, cotton batting; fused, thread painted, machine quilted ● Photo by Gerhard Heidersberger ● Collection of Paul Lamberston, Frederick, Maryland

Preserving Nature

Nature in all her glory surrounds us if we just care enough to look. How can we not be inspired by its beauty? From the translucent wings of the Luna moth to ancient cypress trees, these are nature's gifts. The rate at which so many species are disappearing is alarming. We must remember that man is an animal too and can easily follow other creatures into extinction. I hope in some small way that I am preserving nature in my fiber pieces, for all to see and enjoy for eternity.

Eden

I often think that if I could have lived at another time, I would have joined Charles Darwin on the *HMS Beagle* in the Galapagos Islands. To spend my days exploring, sketching, and taking notes on magnificent creatures would have been a joy.

I opened my blinds this morning so that my cat, Cleopatra, could look out the window and worry the lizards on the sill. A zebra longwing butterfly flitted by, and a dragonfly was poised on the bougainvillea, ready for flight. Moments later, a pair of woodpeckers called to each other in my oak tree: "Good bugs in this old tree," they seemed to say. Out back, having morning coffee on my patio, I watched a crab spider diligently repairing her web. An anhinga, drying his wings after a morning shower, was perched perilously on the very top of a bald cypress tree. A young osprey soon joined the anhinga, momentarily startling him. Two gray squirrels chased each other through the palm trees. And the tiny yellow-breasted warblers that return each winter sang to each other.

Eden, surely. This is why I create my fiber pieces.

NESTOR, A LITTLE GREEN HERON, 2009 ● 23 x 36 x 2 inches
(58.4 x 91.4 x 5.1 cm) ● 100% commercial cottons, batiks,
exotic yarns, quilting and embroidery thread, hand-dyed
cotton thread, buckram, cotton batting; photography, thread
painted, machine couched, hand stitched, machine quilted
● Photo by Gerhard Heidersberger

insects

MICHAEL CUMMINGS ● ZEBRA SWALLOWTAIL, 2001 ● 60 x 60 inches (152.4 x 152.4 cm) ●
100% cotton, cotton blends, linen, rayon; machine sewn, appliquéd ● Quilted by Bonnie Eng
● Photo by Karen Bell

MAGGIE DILLON ● BEES IN THE HIVE, 2010 ●
34 x 34 inches (86.4 x 86.4 cm) ● Batik; thread
work, hand pieced, machine appliquéd ●
Photo by artist

DIANE RUSIN DORAN ● THE GATHERING, 2008
● 43½ x 41½ inches (110.5 x 105.4 cm) ●
100% cotton, 100% silk, pigment ink, fiber-reactive
dye; digital collage, machine quilted ●
Photo by artist

GABRIELLE PAQUIN ● METAMORPHOSIS IN 5D, 2007 ● 51 x 51 inches (129.5 x 129.5 cm) ● Cotton; machine pieced, machine quilted, appliquéd ● Photo by Denis Trimoreau

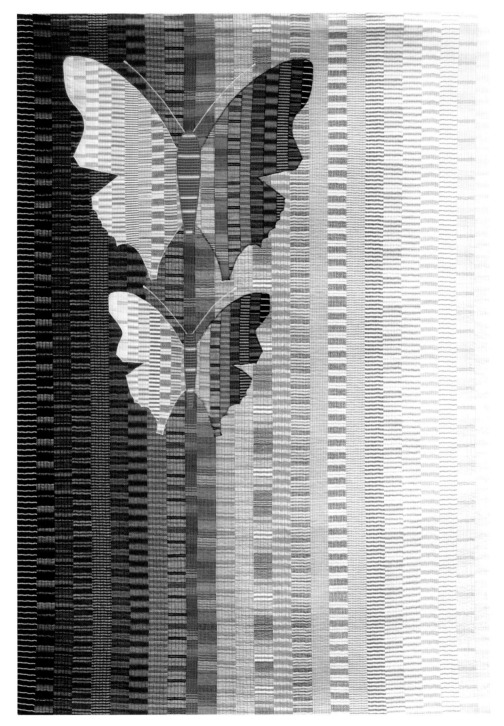

GABRIELLE PAQUIN ● METAMORPHOSIS, 2008 ● 56 x 39 inches (142.2 x 99.1 cm) ●
Cotton; machine pieced, machine appliquéd, machine quilted ● Photo by Denis Trimoreau

JANE SASSAMAN ● NIGHT LIFE, 2006 ● 53 x 42 inches (134.6 x 106.7 cm) ● Cotton fabrics; machine appliquéd, machine quilted
● Photo by Gregory Ganter

BETH MILLER ●
BOGONG MOTHS, 2004 ●
40 x 60 inches (101.6 x 152.4 cm)
● Hand-painted and dyed
cotton, corduroy fabrics, wool
and cotton thread; machine and
hand embroidered, fused appliqué
● Photo by David Paterson

DONNA JUNE KATZ ● SCATTERED
LEAVES WITH PLANETS, 2004 ●
23 x 22 inches (58.4 x 55.9 cm)
● Unbleached muslin, thinned acrylic
paint, whole cloth; hand painted, hand
quilted ● Photo by Tom Van Eynde

RUTH B. MCDOWELL

INSPIRED BY THE WORLD AROUND HER, Ruth B. McDowell creates vibrant images of animals and flowers. While she was an early innovator in the use of mathematical tessellations in pieced patterns and has created large bodies of work that focus on architectural details, forest landscapes, and people, McDowell is best known for her nature pieces. Featuring a wide variety of commercial fabrics, her works are primarily machine pieced using myriad straight and curved seams. In some quilts, these seams are strategically placed to reflect the geometry inherent in the natural world. It is the strength of McDowell's artistic vision that takes these underlying patterns and uses them to create floral studies of supple beauty and animal portraits with tremendous personality.

WITCH HAZEL—JELENA, 2005 ● 80 x 61 inches (20.3 x 154.9 cm) ● Cotton fabric, threads, and batting; machine pieced and quilted ● Photo by David Caras ● Collection of the International Quilt Study Center, University of Nebraska–Lincoln

Rural Massachusetts

I live in a rural hill town in western Massachusetts that has a population of about 1,500 and is covered with forests, brooks, fields, orchards, and farms.

My work is greatly influenced by what I see in the natural world around me. I can look out any window or drive to the post office and see beautiful things every season of the year. If I lived elsewhere, I'd see different things, but I can't imagine living in a city or in most suburbs.

Inspiration

The inspiration for most of my art quilts is a love of nature. In adapting nature to the quilting medium, I try to distill the essence of the subject, leaving out much more than I put in. Each nature quilt becomes an intense exploration of the subject matter.

Something I've seen recently or remember from the past will come to mind as something I'd like to work with as an image. Occasionally, a piece of fabric will spark an idea of a way to tackle an image that has been intriguing me for a while.

Whether I start with a photograph or a drawing, I carefully consider how I can work with that idea within the machine-piecing process and develop a diagram of the individual pieces of fabric that I will need and how

GREAT UNCLE ENOCH, 2009 ● 29½ x 20½ inches (75 x 52.1 cm) ● Cotton fabric, threads, and batting; machine pieced and quilted ● Photo by John Polak

they can be assembled. I have to think about the sewing order while I'm making the drawing and think about how I can use what I have for fabric.

They Are Quilts

Annie Dillard quotes a painter, who, when asked why he painted, replied, "I like the smell of paint." I like the textures and colors and patterns of fabric. It's a very tactile medium. And I find most people respond to quilted textiles in a very intimate way.

My quilts are not trying to be photographs. They are quite unapologetic about being quilts. They are impressionistic in their treatment of natural subject matter, trying to convey my delight in the natural world. My quilts are proud to have come from the tradition of quilt making that so many women have enjoyed.

I am very interested in using the characteristics of the quilt medium as part of the design process. The construction of each quilt becomes a dialogue between the artist and the emerging image. The possibilities and limitations of the piecing process are integral parts of the design. The quilting stitches complete the

transformation of disparate scraps of fabric into a unified whole.

I greatly enjoy employing a variety of cotton fabrics from different sources, different eras, and different cultures. The richness they add to the quilt reflects the variety of the human experience with fibers and our connections to the quilters of the past.

I work simultaneously in several different formats. Many of my art quilts are constructed from full-size drawings, each line on the drawing becoming a seam line between two pieces of cloth. A template copy of the drawing is gradually cut up, with each piece of paper being used as a template for a single piece of fabric. The pieces are then joined by machine to form a pieced top. Other quilts are made in a block style, although the blocks are not usually traditional squares. Tessellations, symmetry, and my fascination with geometry contribute to my block quilts, producing a surface composed of repeating units. Occasionally, both techniques—freehand drawing and repeated blocks—occur in the same piece.

WALLFLOWERS, 2007 ● 48 x 88½ inches (121.9 x 224.8 cm) ● Cotton fabric, threads, and batting; machine pieced and quilted
● Photo by John Polak

I choose the pattern of my quilting stitches to complement each pieced top. I quilt by hand and/or use free-motion machine quilting. The process of adding the linear pattern of quilting stitches to the pieced surface unifies the whole, transforming it into a low relief and adding an extra layer of texture.

Geometry in Nature

I am very interested in structure and sometimes choose a geometrical design to describe that aspect. But because of the way the pieced top is assembled, I can choose some of the major lines or angles of the image to extend from the image across the background/borders of the quilt design. I may choose fabrics in such a way to emphasize the lines, or partly obscure them, as I deem visually correct. The shapes of all of the pieces in a pieced quilt are related in some degree to the architecture of the subject matter. This gives a unity to the quilt that is not available in appliquéd, fused, or painted quilts.

Palette

I only use commercial fabrics, as the whole range of available fabrics gives me a much richer surface than if I restricted myself to just hand dyes, or batiks, or "art fabrics," or painted my own. The auditioning of each and every fabric piece in the context of all the others is the most difficult part of the whole process. It's a challenge to find what I need and fun to work with what is out there. I avoid the printed photo-realistic landscape, rock, and sky fabrics like the plague.

My palette for each piece develops from the fabrics I happen to have at the time and from the way they start to interact with each other as I put them up. I never start with a careful color drawing of a potential quilt. I may have an idea of where I'm going in my head, but it often changes as the fabrics come out to play.

I would be bored to tears to do the same thing all the time. Sometimes, if I've recently made a very subtle quilt with very careful neutrals, I'll go in the opposite direction on the next one and let the colors go wild. The ideal is to make each quilt work as a successful visual composition.

Working Methods

If I work from a photograph, it is a *long* way from the photographic image to what I will use for a plan of

BLUE CLEMATIS, 2008 ● 35 x 31 inches (88.9 x 78.7 cm) ● Cotton fabric, threads, and batting; machine pieced and quilted ● Photo by John Polak

SAWTOOTH TULIP, 2004 ● 35 x 53 inches (88.9 x 134.6 cm) Cotton fabric, threads, and batting; machine pieced and quilted ● Photo by David Caras

ROOSTER, 2009 ● 25½ x 17 inches (64.8 x 43.2 cm) ●
Cotton fabric, threads, and batting; machine pieced and
quilted ● Photo by John Polak

piecing in the quilt. A lot of abstraction will have to be done, many details implied rather than delineated. Choosing which lines to emphasize and at exactly what angles is a careful visual process.

It's much quicker and more pleasant to work with paper and pencils and to draw with my hands than to use a computer drafting program. Designing the piecing can't be done mathematically or with a computer making the choices of the lines, because there are too many careful aesthetic judgments to be made. Making the choices for each seam or line visually is a real art.

In making color choices, I only work with the actual fabrics cut to size. I make choices in the context of having all of the fabric pieces for a quilt pinned into place. Color works entirely differently on a computer screen and at a small size than it does at the real size in actual fabrics. I almost never use solid-color fabric, so working with the actual pieces of fabric is the only way to make the best visual choices.

I've developed a way to use freezer-paper templates, which are adhered to the backs of all of the fabric pieces, and this lets me audition all of the pieces in place and in the context of all of the other pieces before I start to sew.

Appreciating Quilts

I'm proud of my quilts. I think they make strong and beautiful visual statements. People remember my quilts years after they saw them, so they must make a strong connection with other people, too.

Remember to appreciate quilts for what they are. Don't get into prioritizing art versus craft, or ranking "painting" over "fabric pieces," or valuing art by the price it commands, or only looking at the art promoted by the art marketers. Use your eyes and your heart to learn to look and respond.

HIMALAYAN BLUE POPPY, 2003 ● 70½ x 52 inches (179.1 x 132.1 cm) ● Cotton fabric, threads, and batting; machine pieced and quilted ● Photo by David Caras

ELAINE QUEHL

DRAMATIC SCENES ABOUND IN NATURE, but who knew that hostas could be such drama queens? In Elaine Quehl's hands, these reliable garden-filler plants grab center stage, demanding our admiration with their interplay of light and shadow, curve and furl. Quehl dyes her own fabrics to create the full palette needed to capture the range of greens present in each plant and to create the illusion of dappled light common to where they thrive. Seeing each of her pieces as a metaphor for some important aspect of her life, Quehl makes arresting compositions—symphonies in green that show us how to truly see the beauty around us.

HOSTA, 2008 ● 12 x 12 inches (30.5 x 30.5 cm) ●
Hand-dyed cottons; fusible appliqué, artist pencils,
free-motion machine quilted ● Photo by artist ●
Collection of Shirley Neary

Childhood Influences

I was born on a farm in rural southwestern Ontario, close to the village of Wellesley. Growing up somewhat isolated, I had a lot of time to myself for introspection. I also learned how to amuse myself without the activities and distractions that kids in the city have. All of this made it easier for me as an adult to follow my own path and to work alone at home for days and weeks on end. I especially learned to appreciate nature, the rhythms of the seasons, and the cycles of life. As a child, I collected monarch butterfly cocoons off sheaves of grain, watching them hatch, then protecting them until their wings dried and they were able to take flight.

Turning to Fiber

My mother, grandmothers, and great-grandmothers were all quilters, so I grew up surrounded by traditional quilts. Although I probably took the quilts very much for granted, I started taking classes to learn traditional quilt-making methods in 1996 as a way to cope with losing my mother to Alzheimer's. I didn't intentionally begin to create art in fabric but got hooked on the peace and calm I felt while I was creating. My quilt-making journey took me to a place I didn't even know existed until I saw art quilts at a show for the first time. I became determined to develop my artistic skills in this medium, since I already had a foundation in using fabric and thread.

VAGABOND SONG, 2010 ● 20 x 24 inches (50.8 x 61 cm) ● Hand-dyed cottons; fused collage, thread painted, free-motion machine quilted ● Photo by artist

STANDING OVATION, 2010 ● 24 x 56 inches (61 x 142.2 cm) ● Hand-dyed cottons; fusible appliqué, free-motion machine quilted
● Photo by artist

Metaphors for Life

I think we don't always know why we make a piece or what it means at the time, but during the process and sometimes even after the piece is finished, I can always see that what I have made can be a metaphor for what is happening in my emotional life. For example, it was easy to see the unfurling hostas as a metaphor for my own life. I created my first hosta piece, *Opening Act*, when I was in my early 40s, a time when I was starting to grow comfortable in my over-40 skin and to accept myself, imperfections and all. I was coming out of my shell of shyness, largely as a result of my successes in the quilting world, the experience of lecturing to large groups, and leading workshops. The hostas represent that growth: stretching, reaching, learning, and maturing. I made *In the Act* in 2010. To me, it seems an apt metaphor for someone who is in full swing with her art quilt career. My most recent piece, *Standing Ovation*, celebrates a hosta patch in full maturity and my own successful year, in which I was able to make a living as an artist and teacher.

Why Hostas?

In June 2006 I was attending a conference in Prince Edward Island, Canada. It had been raining off and on for a few days, and I noticed the lushness of the hosta leaves as they were unfurling. I took a few photos and think they are among the best pictures I have ever taken. Those images kept on speaking to me, and I was compelled to make *Opening Act* as a result. I was very happy with the piece and could easily see how the unfolding of the hosta leaves seemed a metaphor for my own life.

I now notice hostas everywhere I go and have probably shot a few thousand images of them in the last four years. I adore the value contrasts, the juxtaposition of highlights and shadows, and the drama that results. Hostas seem the perfect plants on which to conduct a study of light and shadow. The curves and fullness reflect the sun's light but also cast shadows along the leaves below. I associate their green color with life itself.

PEONY, 2008 ● 36 x 46 inches (91.4 x 116.8 cm) ●
Hand-dyed cottons; fusible appliqué, free-motion machine
quilted ● Photo by artist

SEEING RED, 2009 ● 47½ x 60 inches (120.7 x 152.4 cm) ●
Hand-dyed cottons; fusible appliqué, free-motion machine
quilted ● Photo by artist

Our Garden

We do have a sort of haphazard (mostly perennial) flower garden at our house, and my husband is in charge of it. Now that I'm a full-time artist, teacher, and dyer, I'm afraid I haven't much time for gardening. *Standing Ovation* and my poppy pieces were inspired by plants from our garden.

Having said that, if a leaf, a flower, or a tree speaks to me, I don't discriminate based on where it is growing. We love to travel, and I take photographs wherever I go. I visit the botanical gardens in every city we visit. It is often when I am traveling that I feel most inspired. I find that new surroundings heighten my senses and awareness and make me notice things I might take for granted if they were part of my everyday environment.

Color

I think my colors and values are often an exaggerated version of reality—the lights get lighter and the darks get darker.

This provides the visual drama I am striving for in my work. Sometimes I can't decide if I am happiest when my work looks like what I am representing or if I am happiest when it doesn't. I would say my preference is for abstracted reality. When I am depicting a full leaf or tree or flower, I think my work appears more realistic, but when I crop a composition and choose to emphasize the lines or shapes of only a portion of it, then it tends to be more abstract. After I made my second foliage piece, I recall being asked if I was ever going to work in anything but green. The answer is yes, but I'm still not finished with green.

Working Methods

I usually begin with one of my photographs for inspiration. I am very selective in which photographs I use; I tried for two years until I got poppy photos that I felt I could use. I am particularly drawn to photos with lots of depth, highlights, and shadows. Using a photo as my guide, I

UNFURLING, 2009 ● 12 x 12 inches (30.5 x 30.5 cm)
Hand-dyed cottons; fusible appliqué, artist pencils, free-motion machine quilted ● Photo by artist

create a line drawing that indicates every color and value change I see. The drawing is enlarged into my working pattern. I then transfer my pattern to the background fabric or build my flower or tree on a muslin foundation so it can later be auditioned on potential backgrounds. I don't feel that I have to adhere strictly to the pattern, however, and I will often make changes in the design right up to the final stages. I often liken the process of building my pieces to painting with brushstrokes of fabric.

I am also a dyer, so I have a huge stash of fabric in many colors and values—particularly green! I pull pieces of the fabric out, line them up by value, and evaluate whether I need to dye any additional fabrics to realize my vision. I use my own hand-dyed fabric because the mottled fabric that results from low-water immersion dyeing methods reads like dappled light.

I want my work to have enough impact that it grabs viewers from across the room and invites them to investigate more closely. I want them to see nature's drama. Mostly, I want them to be moved, to experience the range of emotions I felt when I encountered the plant that has inspired me.

IN THE ACT, 2010 ● 47 x 22 inches (119.4 x 55.9 cm) ● Hand-dye cottons; fusible appliqué, free-motion machine quilted ● Photo by artist

BRANCHING OUT, 2010 ● 28 x 20½ inches (71.1 x 52.1 cm) ● Hand-dyed cottons and velvets; fused collage, thread painted, free-motion machine quilted ● Photo by artist

flowers II

BETH WHEELER ● LABYRINTH, 2008 ● 30 x 24 x 1 inches (76.2 x 61 x 2.5 cm)
● Cotton twill, fleece batting, photograph; computer manipulated, printed, free-
motion machine stitched ● Photo by artist

DEBORAH SCHWARTZMAN
● JUICY FRUIT, 2003 ●
38 x 58½ inches (96.5 x 148.6 cm)
● Silk, cotton, rayon,
organza, polyester, silk
thread; hand stamped and
dyed, machine pieced,
hand and machine quilted,
machine embroidered,
embellished, fused ●
Photo by John Carlano

RITA STEFFENSON ●
TWILIGHT, 2008 ● 79 x
108 x ¼ inches (200.7 x 274.3
x 0.6 cm) ● 100% cotton,
fabrics dyed and painted by
the artist; machine appliquéd, machine quilted ●
Photo by Kevin Steffenson

SMADAR KNOBLER ●
MAJESTIC LEYA, 2010
● 25 x 32 x 4 inches
(63.5 x 81.3 x 10.2 cm)
● 100% silk, 100% cotton,
paint, wire; machine pieced and
quilted ● Photo by artist

KATHLEEN MCCABE ●
PROTEA, 2009 ● 31 x 41 inches
(78.7 x 104.1 cm) ● 100% cotton,
commercial fabrics; fused and
machine appliquéd, machine
quilted ● Photo by Phil Imming

ELSBETH NUSSER-LAMPE ● STRUGGLE, 2010 ● 43 x 43 inches (109.2 x 109.2 cm) ● Cotton and silk; hand dyed, machine appliquéd, machine quilted ● Photo by artist

JUANITA YEAGER ● LILIES IN BLOOM, 2009 ● 45 x 38 inches (114.3 x 96.5 cm) ● Silk broadcloth; dye painted, machine quilted ● Photo by artist

SUSAN BRUBAKER KNAPP ● FRECKLES, 2010 ● 35 x 24½ x ¼ inches (88.9 x 62.3 x 0.6 cm) ●
White cotton fabric, acrylic textile paint, cotton threads, wool polyester batting; whole-cloth painted,
free-motion machine quilted ● Photo by artist

DOTTIE MOORE

TREES—THEIR STRENGTH AND POWER, singularity and majesty—call to us from Dottie Moore's artwork. A deeply spiritual, meditative practice leads her work from its humble beginnings in plain white cloth through painting sessions that result in a rich palette of colors. Fabrics are then cut, appliquéd, and stitched, then backed and quilted a second time. Adding an array of embroidered details, Moore creates scenes filled with symbolism and a deep sense of peace. Each part of the landscape—tree, cloud, stream, bird, mountain—has a meaning beyond its physical characteristics. Each is precisely placed in position because it is meant to be there. The pathways beckon us toward a deeper understanding of our place within the natural world.

RED TREE, 1997 ● 36 x 24 inches (91.4 x 61 cm) ●
Hand-painted cotton fabric, cotton batting; machine appli-
quéd, hand and machine embroidered, machine quilted ●
Photo by Michael Harrison

Why Trees?

My earliest memories of trees include the sweet gum tree in the front yard of my childhood home and the mimosa tree in the front yard of a neighbor. The sweet gum's prickly balls and the soft, fuzzy pink flowers of the mimosa tree stirred my imagination, and I received them as gifts for my make-believe world. Throughout my life there have been many trees that have called to me and remain in my memory bank today.

Trees are my symbol for life, and I find messages in every one that I quilt. Trees teach me how to dance the dance of opposites. They grow deep roots to explore the dark places of earth, so that their branches can reach for the light. This reminds me to balance my own life by nurturing my inner journey as much as the outer one.

Trees are flexible. They know how to endure life's challenges and thrive in difficult environments. I love the way trees bend and sway with the forces of life and dance in stormy weather. They know how to surrender to the seasons. They willingly release their leaves, strip themselves bare, and rest, so that they can be reborn again each spring. This is how they stand in their fullness and live long lives.

The endless variety of trees reminds me that diversity is what makes the world beautiful, and that the

HER ROOTS GROW DEEP, 2009 ● 36 x 24 inches (91.4 x 61 cm) ● Hand-painted cotton fabric, cotton batting; machine appliquéd, hand and machine embroidered, machine quilted ● Photo by Michael Harrison

uniqueness of every person is to be celebrated. Trees are strong and centered in their spots on earth and remind me to do the same. They remind me that "being" is enough, and that I am to show up for my life by being present and alive in every moment.

Early Influences

I come from a lineage of women who sewed. My earliest memory of cloth and thread is from age five. I remember turning the wheel of my mother's treadle sewing machine so that I could watch the needle go up and down. I learned all the needle arts as a girl growing up in the South in the 1940s and 50s, and when I was older I made most of my clothes.

In 1968, my love of fiber led me to weaving, which was my passion for several years. My art quilting began spontaneously when I co-curated an exhibit of woven work with a friend. There was an empty space that needed to be filled, so I went home that night and made my first quilt. The central image of this quilt was a tree. That was in 1980, and I have never looked back.

Spiritual Nature of Art

My artwork *is* my spiritual work. It is meditation. It is the pathway to my unconscious. Both the process of making art and the images that emerge from this process feed my soul.

THE CALL, 2009 ● 41 x 60 inches (104.1 x 152.4 cm) ● Hand-painted cotton fabric, cotton batting; machine appliquéd, hand and machine embroidered, machine quilted ● Photo by Michael Harrison

It didn't start out this way. In the beginning, I just wanted to make things. The awareness of why came with the practice. My logical mind kept telling me to get an art degree, read more art books, or at least take a few workshops in art. However, my soul nudged me to buy one more spiritual, philosophical, or self-help book, and to take another yoga, Feldenkrais, or tai-chi class. It is my soul that attends these metaphysical lectures and studies with energy workers.

Gradually, I have developed a deep personal belief system that guides me. I have decided to follow my heart, deepen my personal self-awareness, and stay with my commitment to always grow and change. I trust this process to flow into my art. I believe that the more I simplify my life, the more my imagination expands.

Art as Meditation

I am a great believer in the power of the "beginner's mind," so I try to begin every piece as if I have never quilted before. This is art. I want it to emerge from the void. I want to begin with nothing and create an image that satisfies me.

My process begins with my morning practices. Before I speak to anyone, including my husband, I spend several hours in the early morning renewing myself and getting to know me—the new me that has arrived from a night of sleep. This personal time might include yoga or other forms of movement, meditation, journal writing, reading, making a plan for my day, or simple contemplation when I sit and allow fresh thoughts to enter.

Working Intuitively

Here is how *The Call* developed. On the day that I started this quilt, I entered my studio curious about what might emerge. I opened the box where I store scraps and leftover textured fabric from previous quilts. I had a piece of embroidered green grass, which had been discarded from the large commissioned piece that I had just completed. Not wanting to waste so much stitching, I began with the grass, which was quickly followed by a large piece of painted sky. I loved the clouds in this painted sky and thought that this could be a very simple design focusing on them. However, I then discovered a large tree that I had discarded from another quilt, and I liked the way it took over and became the central focus. At this point, I thought that I was content. I didn't want to clutter the quilt.

WISDOM KEEPERS, 2006 ● 20 x 20 inches (50.8 x 50.8 cm) Hand-painted cotton fabric, cotton batting; machine appliquéd, hand and machine embroidered, machine quilted ● Photo by Michael Harrison

TREE, 2000 ● 75 x 81 inches (190.5 x 205.7 cm) ● Hand-painted cotton fabric, cotton batting; machine appliquéd, hand and machine embroidered, machine quilted ● Photo by Michael Harrison

Dottie Moore

WHOLENESS, 1995 ● 36 x 36 inches (91.4 x 91.4 cm) ●
Hand-painted cotton fabric, cotton batting; machine appli-
quéd, hand and machine embroidered, machine quilted
● Photo by Michael Harrison ● Collection of Meridian
Educational Research Center, Atlanta, Georgia

I always want to "see beyond," so without any conscious thought I added the feeling of a window in this quilt. The depth that the window created satisfied something deep inside of me. The smaller tree and the stream were also added to please my unconscious mind, and they helped to balance the design. The decision for the heavily stitched foreground came about in the same intuitive way. And all of this was created before the raven/crow entered my mind. She/he was spontaneously added last, as well as the three birds in the distance.

How Place Has Affected Subject Matter

Where I live definitely influences my work, but the influence is not as direct from nature as one might imagine when looking at my representational work. When I lived in the silence of the mountains in Tennessee and walked among the wildflowers that grew in the woods, I tried to capture what I saw. My first art quilts were images of wildflowers, and my early landscapes were filled with mountain ranges, using a color palette that changed with the seasons.

In 1987, we moved to South Carolina, and my studio is now in the city. The only remnants of inspiration from those early years of living near the mountains are the trees around our new home. My inspiration has gone inward. I rely on my feelings for inspiration. Images of mountains and trees continue to appear in my quilts, but they are now symbols.

Growing Importance of Symbolism

I interpret my quilts symbolically, in the same way I interpret my night dreams. Trees, mountains, streams, pathways, clouds, and colors reflect what is happening in my life and what I need to say. My mandala quilts are meditative images that also weave in and out of my work, and sometimes my expressions are abstract. I enjoy creating these pieces, but the symbolic messages that I create with my nature symbols satisfy a deeper part of my psyche. My intention is to "show up" for each creation, so that my unconscious has a place to express itself.

I never quilt particular trees or mountain ranges. I am not interested in capturing anything but the feeling of my symbols. Trees come into my work only when and if *they* chose to enter. The trees in my quilts are versions of *me*.

MIST, 2002 ● 43 x 41 inches (109.2 x 104.1 cm) ● Hand-
painted cotton fabric, cotton batting; machine appliquéd,
hand and machine embroidered, machine quilted ●
Photo by Michael Harrison ● Collection of Bob Moore

HUMMINGBIRD MYSTERIES, 2010 ● 56 x 49 inches (142.2 x 124.5 cm) ● Hand-painted cotton fabric, cotton batting; machine appliquéd, hand and machine embroidered, machine quilted ● Photo by Michael Harrison ● Collection of Creative Art Services

● Dottie Moore

NANCY G. COOK

DELICATELY INKED LINES AND GLOWING COLORS highlight the beauty of the tree seed pods and berries found in Nancy G. Cook's work. Drawn to the infinite variety of form and function present in these often overlooked portions of a tree's life cycle, Cook sees them as metaphors for human life and interaction. Insect and wind damage show the dignity of a life lived in service to others, while the pods' diversity illustrates the importance of tolerance as a long-term survival strategy. Not as showy as flowers or abundant as leaves, seed pods occur in an amazing array of colors and structures. Each one is lovingly detailed and celebrated in Cook's artwork. Dense machine quilting lines add sculptural design elements, while hand embroidery highlights carefully selected elements.

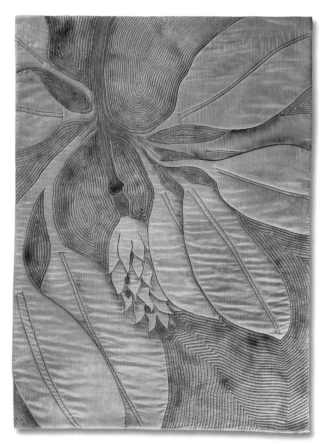

SOUTHERN HERITAGE, 2008 ● 35 x 26 inches (88.9 x 66 cm)
● Cotton, ink; whole cloth, hand-guided machine quilted, stenciled, hand embroidered ● Photo by Mitchell Kearney

My Love of Fiber

Fiber has always been the medium I prefer. I love the look and feel of fabrics and thread. They hold very strong memories for me of when my mother created all my clothing. One or the other of us would find a great piece of cloth, and together we would decide what to create from it.

My fiber work is informed by the traditions of both quilting and botanical illustration. It combines my passions for nature, texture, color, and women's work as art. I work with fabric because I love it—the look of it, the feel of it, and its historical association with comfort and security. I love the way the machine-quilted line creates both line and texture as *bas relief* sculpture. I find that these textures are immensely pleasurable to my eye. When I create a top, it seems flat and unfinished until it comes alive with quilting and embroidery.

Living in the South

I was born on my grandparents' tobacco farm in Virginia. I now live in the suburbs of Charlotte, North Carolina, surrounded by trees and wildlife. While where I live has influenced the topical content of my work, it has not influenced my choice of medium or broader aspects of my work. I have always been drawn to nature and the outdoors, so using it for imagery is

LIGUSTRUM TWILIGHT, 2009 ● 36 x 25 inches (91.4 x 63.5 cm) ● Cotton, ink; whole cloth, hand-guided machine quilted, stenciled, hand embroidered ● Photo by David Ramsey

ANKLE TWISTER II, 2009 ● 9 x 9 inches (22.9 x 22.9 cm)
● Cotton, ink; whole cloth, hand-guided machine quilted,
stenciled, hand embroidered ● Photo by artist ●
Collection of the International Quilt Study Center and
Museum, Lincoln, Nebraska

BURFORD HOLLY, 2009 ● 8 x 10 inches (20.3 x 25.4 cm)
● Cotton, ink; whole cloth, hand-guided machine quilted,
stenciled, hand embroidered ● Photo by artist

what I know best. Currently, I am working on a series featuring native plants of the South, but I might be working on desert plants if I lived in the Southwest.

Tree Seeds

Recently, I have fallen in love with tree seeds; the variety of reproductive strategies is fascinating, as their seeds are dispersed by wind, water, or animals. It is intriguing that an outside force must help disperse the beginnings of the next generation.

My current series, *Seed Play*, focuses on tree seeds and fruits as metaphors for life's riches that come with maturity. Part of my effort is to examine and reveal what differentiates one tree species' seeds from another. In that context, I strive to illustrate that each individual is unique and wonderful by focusing with admiration and care on a part of the tree that is often overlooked. The seeds' many different forms emphasize the importance of diversity for survival and, by extension, illustrate the importance of diversity in individuals. Life has evolved to favor diversity within a species as a survival mechanism. I believe that we put our species in peril when we fail to recognize and value diversity.

The Beauty of Imperfection

Perfection can seem cold and unreal. Most of my specimens show damage from insects or weather. This shows that they have truly lived, which seems more interesting and more real. All of us have imperfections, and I want to convey my acceptance of imperfections as beautiful reminders that life goes on.

Sketching and Photography

I use a combination of camera imagery and sketches from life for my work. The camera helps me think through design layout by allowing quicker position changes of the specimen than sketching does. On the other hand, sketching helps me to really see and study the piece for the details that I want to capture. It is not uncommon for me to make half a dozen sketches and a dozen or more photos.

The computer allows me to copy photos and crop them for design purposes, to make small copies of the final design, to do color studies before inking the design, and to enlarge a small design to the final size. The computer helps remove some of the labor intensiveness of the work.

Color Choice

I choose fabrics based on the mood or atmosphere or emotion I want for a piece. To me art is communicating, and colors communicate emotion. For example, for the piece *After the Frost* (not pictured), I wanted a fabric color that conveyed the coolness of winter yet hinted at the color of the ripe persimmons.

Sometimes realistic colors do a good job, sometimes they do not. For instance, the colors of the seed pod in *Ankle Twister* are unrealistic but suggest the mystery of life. In this case, I showcased a seed pod that is both familiar to and often hated by many people in the South but is rarely seen as an object of beauty. I think that part of this lack of appreciation is because of the dull color of the pods, so I changed the colors to help people pay more attention and to see the beautiful forms that are revealed by looking closely.

Inking

Southern Heritage was an early piece in the *Seed Play* series. Fascinated by the seed pods on the magnolia tree, I collected a specimen and made many sketches and photographs of it. It always takes multiple trials to get the image ready for production. I complete the design on paper in a small size—about 5 x 7 inches (12.7 x 17.7 cm)—scan it into the computer, and then crop and rotate it until the image has the design components that I want.

JUNIPERUS, 2009 ● 26 x 37 inches (66 x 94 cm) ● Cotton, ink; whole cloth, hand-guided machine quilted, stenciled, hand embroidered ● Photo by David Ramsey

The final image was enlarged to full size and drawn on freezer paper. Then I selected from my stash of fabrics hand-dyed by Heide Stoll Weber. I use her fabrics because of the sensuous way the colors gently move from one to another. I put my design onto the fabric with semi-transparent inks, so the quality of the background fabric would not overpower the imagery. In this case, I selected a green fabric that suggested the magnolia's evergreen leaves and had a lighter yellow area where I could use orange-red ink for the seed pod.

I cut out freezer-paper templates with a utility knife. I layered the ink colors, beginning with the lightest areas. The color of the background fabric serves as highlights in the pieces, much like paper does when painting with watercolors. Sometimes I ink the imagery onto the fabric; at other times I ink the background so the imagery is revealed. Once the entire image has been inked, I check for areas that are not clear and may reinforce lines to add depth of color or shadows.

After heat-setting it with an iron, I put the quilt sandwich together with close thread basting. I machine-quilted the long lines first, then outlined the imagery throughout. Stitching adds additional dimension. For the background, I used a machine-quilt line that is a variant of Hawaiian echo quilting.

I will use up to 20 different thread colors to quilt a piece and use variegated threads if they have the right color and value. The thread colors add dimension by

KOUSA: A NEW DOGWOOD'S IN TOWN, 2010 ● 36 x 36 inches (91.4 x 91.4 cm) ●
Cotton, ink; whole cloth, hand-guided machine quilted, stenciled, hand embroidered ●
Photo by artist

highlighting and shading but rarely contrast strongly with the main image. Thread may cool an area and make it seem to recede, or warm an area and make it seem to come forward; it may also make an area seem more rounded.

Once the machine quilting was done, I added highlights and details with simple embroidery stitches with cotton embroidery thread. Again, the thread color will generally blend, or it might add an accent color that moves your eye around the piece. In *Southern Heritage*, I put in small, dark-brown tips to the seed areas and added seed stitching for the details on the stem just below the pod.

Look Closely

I find the interconnected web of life to be endlessly fascinating, and I like working with one small piece of it to unravel some of life's wonders. My work has unintentionally become autobiographical: I began creating autumnal images at the same time that I became aware that I came to my art in the autumn of my life. Fortunately, it seems to be a Southern autumn that is prolonged. Looking, really looking, reveals a great deal of beauty all around us and within us as well.

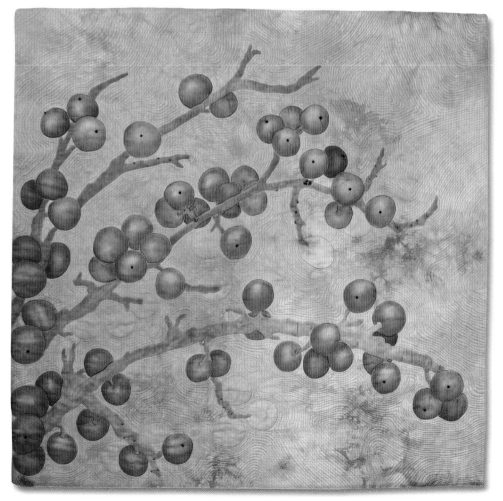

MOCKINGBIRD'S LARDER, 2010 ● 36 x 36 inches (91.4 x 91.4 cm) ● Cotton, ink; whole cloth, hand-guided machine quilted, stenciled, hand embroidered ● Photo by artist

trees

CATHERINE TIMM ● QUIET WINTER FOREST, 2009 ● 40 x 48 inches (101.6 x 121.9 cm) ● 100% cotton fabric, fabric paint, cotton and polyester threads, yarns, dryer sheets, cheesecloth, 50/50 cotton-bamboo batting; machine appliquéd and stitched ● Photo by Jeremiah Lapointe

MARTHA COLE ● SCOTS PINE, 2009 ● 48 x 48 inches (121.9 x 121.9 cm) ● Digital image on cotton, archival pigment-based inks, unbleached cotton, fabric paints, assorted threads, polyester batting; whole-cloth quilting ● Photo by Carolyn Pihach

LESLIE GABRIËLSE ● TREE I, 2006
● 63 x 88⁹⁄₁₆ inches (160 x 224.9 cm) ●
Fabric, acrylic paint; hand sewn
● Photo by artist

RASA MAURAGIS ●
DESOLATION, 2005 ●
59 x 59 inches (149.9 x 149.9 cm)
Hand-dyed and rusted cotton,
chiffon, puff paint; machine and
hand quilted using fly and stem
stitches ● Photo by artist

KAREN SCHULZ ● DEEP INTO SUMMER: FIRST FALL, 2006 ● 36 x 52 inches (91.4 x 132.1 cm) ● 100% cotton, silk, nylon netting; fused, machine pieced, appliquéd, quilted, hand dyed ● Photo by PRS Associates

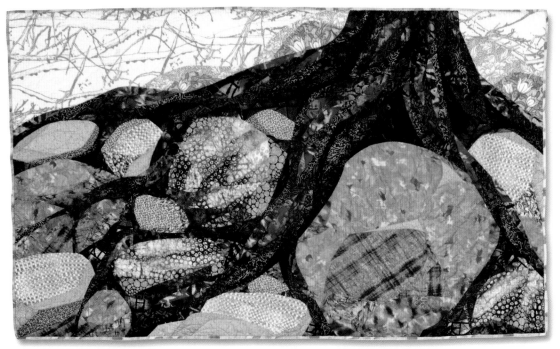

LINDA BEACH ● TENACITY, 2009 ● 36 x 59 inches (91.4 x 149.9 cm) ● 100% cotton fabric and batting, cotton and synthetic threads; machine pieced, free-motion machine quilted ● Photo by Danny Daniels

KATHY BROWN ● PROUD AND STRONG, 2008 ● 67 x 36½ x 2½ inches
(170.2 x 92.7 x 6.4 cm) ● Cotton, silks, synthetics, fabric dye, silk and acrylic paints;
hand and machine pieced, hand and machine appliquéd, hand and machine embroidered, stump work, hand quilted ● Photo by Peter Hurt

JOANNA O'NEILL ● THE WHITE TREE, 2009 ● 24 x 24 inches (61 x 61 cm) 100% cotton, paint; raw-edge bonded appliqué, machine quilted ● Photo by Simon O'Neill

CAROL WATKINS ● ROOTED IN FANTASY II, 2009 ● 25 x 22½ inches (63.5 x 57.2 cm) ● Original photographs, cotton fabric, molding paste, rayon thread; digital processes, inkjet printed, machine pieced, appliquéd, free-motion stitched ● Photo by Ken Sanville

BARBARA BARRICK MCKIE

CHARACTERIZED BY A WONDERFUL OP-ART EFFECT in shades of blue, Barbara Barrick McKie's **Fanfare for an Orange** (2001) features 12 computer-scanned images of an orange as it's being peeled and eaten. To make the piece, McKie peeled an actual orange and placed it on her scanner stage by stage in order to record its disappearance. The background is machine quilted in thousands of tiny orange circles. This combination of realism and abstraction is typical of McKie's work. While the focus of each piece is usually based on one of her photographs, the settings are abstract or fantastical, so that the animal, flower, or still life is brought directly to our attention. We see every detail of the petal as the flower unfolds, or gaze directly into a fawn's gentle eye as he looks up from a nap. McKie's disperse-dye printing technique renders everything in clear, sharp focus, while her meticulous machine quilting provides texture and context. If you have a chance to see her work in person, ask to see the back of a piece, where the image depicted on the front is precisely mirrored in a quilted silhouette.

MOMMY AND ME, 2008 ● 33½ x 33 x ½ inches ● (85.1 x 83.8 x 1.3 cm) ● Disperse-dyed polyester, wool batting, cotton backing, rayon thread, digital imagery; free-motion embroidered, quilted, machine appliquéd, trapunto ● Photo by artist

Living in the Woods

My first interaction with animals was watching the squirrels and birds that visited the feeders outside my windows. Then there were two baby deer, which were born on our property. I made a quilt of one of them when I was able to photograph it. We chose our current home because of the natural environment.

My floral series started on my way back from the Quilt Surface Design Symposium in 1995. Driving along a country lane, I spotted some daylilies growing beside a farm. I stopped to take a picture. That photograph rekindled my interest in flowers (I was a biology major in college). Having already begun exploring how to put images from my camera into my work, I hid a few "real" photographic flowers amongst the appliquéd ones in a lilies-of-the-field pattern. Since then, I've explored many ways to combine realism and abstraction in my quilts.

Culmination of Life's Paths

I feel that I am consolidating my whole life in my art. I've had many careers, including research microbiologist, bridal gown designer/manufacturer, homebuilder,

AFTERNOON OF A FAWN, 2010 ● 30 x 32 x ½ inches (76.2 x 81.3 x 1.3 cm) ● Disperse-dyed polyester, wool batting, cotton backing, rayon thread, digital imagery; free-motion embroidered, quilted, machine appliquéd, trapunto ● Photo by artist

THE HARE'S VERSION, 2009 ● 41¾ x 41 x ¾ inches (106.1 x 104.1 x 1.9 cm) ● Disperse-dyed polyester, wool batting, cotton backing; digital printing, trapunto, free-motion thread painted, free-motion quilted ● Photo by artist

I'M WATCHING YOU, 2010 ● 27½ x 33 x ¾ inches (69.9 x 83.8 x 1.9 cm) ● Disperse-dyed polyester, wool batting, thread, cotton backing; thread painted, trapunto, free-motion machine appliquéd and quilted ● Photo by artist

computer consultant, and finally—my favorite—art quilter. My interest in art started with photography, and it still is a strong starting point both for inspiration and for inclusion in my work. Surface design and the surprises that result continue to sustain my interest in experimenting with fiber and what can be achieved by combining various methods in a unique way.

Use of Camera and Computer

I take lots of photographs, many of animals, but also of flowers that I grow and encounter on my trips. I select one or more photos that inspire me at that particular time to do a work of art. I then edit the image using Photoshop, blowing the image up as large as I want the final quilt to be. I often make the background more abstract or create a special surface-designed fabric for the background.

I divide this new photo image into several overlapping sections, so that each section can fit onto my heat press, which is limited to just short of 16 x 20 inches (40.6 x 50.8 cm). I print the photo sections onto a special paper using disperse dye (also called sublimation dye). I then use my heat press to print it to polyester or another synthetic fabric, since it doesn't work on natural fibers.

Using fusible on the back of each section, I overlap the fabric sections and press the fabrics onto a thin but very stable batting. For the quilts that need to be thread-painted (most of the recent animal quilts), I then sew through the front and batting of the animal parts of the quilt using colors similar to the original photo. I use really tight free-motion stitching to give the effect of hair or fur. I then put several layers of puffy wool batting behind the animal to create a trapunto effect in this area, quilting only around critical areas.

I generally do not thread-paint flowers, but I have used the trapunto layers. I use the same color of rayon thread on the bobbin as on the top in order to make a silhouette of the design on the back of the quilt.

Disperse Dyes

When I began making quilts, I researched different ways of printing and turned to the experts—screenprinters. In 1994 or 1995, I bought a printer that printed both cotton dye and sublimation dye, but the software at the time couldn't really control the sublimation dyes, so I used the cotton dye and the fabrics were stiff. Eventually, I started using disperse dyes, which left the hand of the fabric as soft as it had been initially.

I'm probably one of few people who still uses this method, because the dyes are very pricey. Initially, I used polyester satin, but I found that polyester crepe creates an even sharper image with a nice hand and brighter colors.

Constant Experimentation

Recently, I switched to a more UV-resistant fusible, but I'm also testing all of my fusible brands by creating swatches using different products and placing them in bright sunlight. It's now been over three years, and I have not seen any deterioration of the fabric with fusibles versus the control versions. However, I do see the threads fading on all of the fabrics, including the controls. I've also tested the UV-resistant dyes in normal home lighting and there has been little or no change in the colors or the fabrics. I also test and compare different brands of fusible, dyes, and threads to find products that best produce the effects I want. I'm interested in doing these experiments because of my scientific background.

Intrepid Traveler

My husband and I travel frequently, both in this country and abroad. I always take my camera when I travel in order to photograph interesting flowers and animals and people. Sometimes I combine photos from different parts of the world: one of my latest quilts, *The Hare's Version* is a combination of a tortoise from the Galapagos, a hare from Michigan, and the sky from California.

MANDARIN DUCK, 2010 ● 22¼ x 33½ x ½ inches (56.5 x 85.1 x 1.3 cm) ● Disperse-dyed polyester print, wool batting, cotton backing, rayon thread; trapunto, thread painted, machine appliquéd and quilted ● Photo by artist

PEACOCK PRIDE, 2009 ● 32¼ x 22½ x ½ inches
(81.9 x 57.2 x 1.3 cm) ● Disperse-dyed polyester crepe,
hand-dyed cotton border, cotton backing, wool batting;
machine quilted, free-motion machine embroidered,
trapunto, machine appliquéd ● Photo by artist

WHITE-THROATED SPARROW, 2010 ● 29¾ x 45¾ x ½
inches (75.6 x 116.2 x 1.3 cm) ● Disperse-dyed polyester,
wool batting, cotton backing, rayon thread, digital imagery;
free-motion embroidered, quilted, machine appliquéd, trapunto ● Photo by artist

Why Art Quilts?

My grandmother was a member of a very traditional
quilting bee. I started sewing in seventh grade and have
been creative in this area ever since, beginning with
designing my own clothing.

I taught myself quilting in 1971 when there weren't any
books or magazines to teach you how. I started making
original quilts for my bed and in 1974 made art quilts
for the wall. I actually studied painting later but wasn't
as comfortable with it as with designing using my
sewing machine and my own imagery on fabric.

Changes in the Art Quilt World

Back in 1974, when I started doing art quilts for the
wall, I was relatively unique and was published in many
traditional quilt publications, but now there are many
more venues for art quilts. More people from all over
the world have taken up quilting, and that has also
added to the number of art quilters. Many painters and
other artists have taken up art quilting, and there are
also more people who are doing digital work in art quilts.

Overall, I think the abstract art quilt has been getting more and more attention. Back in 1999, I was
juried into Quilt National, but because of the increased
focus on abstract art in quilting, I've not gotten into
this venue again, even though my work has gotten
much better. However, I've twice been juried into Quilt
Visions, including 2010.

Recurring Themes

I like to take a starting point such as a photograph, a
piece of fabric, or a stone and let it suggest to me what
to do with it. As the creation takes shape, I react to
what I see and add as the piece suggests itself to me.
Characteristics of my work include strong texture,
contrast, and either nature's colors or vibrant color contrasts with a rhythmic movement that comes from an
inner musical sense.

I hope viewers get a chuckle from my work, or want to
pet the animals, or just enjoy the beauty of the flowers.
I want them to be able to observe more of the beauty
that is our natural world and look at it with a new sense
of awe and inspiration.

CAUGHT IN THE ACT, 2010 ● 29 x 32½ x ½ inches (73.7 x 82.6 x 1.3 cm) ● Disperse-dyed polyester, wool batting, cotton backing, rayon thread; thread painted, trapunto, free-motion machine appliquéd and quilted ● Photo by artist

PATRICIA GOULD

THE SHEER SIZE OF THE ROCKS AND ICEBERGS in Patricia Gould's work is awe-inspiring. Their immense scale creates a sense of overwhelming grandeur. The nuanced color gradations and the interplay of subtle shadows combine to form a visual symphony. Based on photos taken throughout her extensive worldwide travels and in her beloved New Mexican high deserts, her works combine a variety of appliqué, paint, and dye techniques to capture the beauty of these lithic and icy masterpieces. Using commercial and hand-dyed fabrics, Gould over-dyes, paints, thread paints, and uses paint sticks to design a variety of effects, adding layers of paint at several stages of construction so that her works truly capture the sense of each natural formation's power. Crystal-clear skies form the backdrop to these ancient colossal monuments. Their enduring strength is a reminder of how ephemeral our own lives are in comparison. Their sublime magnificence is a call to care for the planet.

ANCIENT OWACHOMO, 2008 ● 32 x 30 inches (81.3 x 76.2 cm) ● Hand-painted and commercial cotton, hand-marbled paper, acrylic paint, ink; fused appliqué, free-motion quilted ● Photo by artist ● Permanent Collection of the New Mexico Arts Division, Art in Public Places Program

Wanderlust

I grew up in a small village on Long Island's South Shore. I spent most of my first 39 years living a stone's throw from an ocean. I grew up with the salt air in my lungs, braving the violent surf from the age of five, so water is in my blood.

Due to the wanderlust instilled by my parents, I have been traveling since 1955. When I was only nine months old, my parents packed the four kids into a Mercury station wagon hauling a 27-foot trailer and we visited almost all the national parks. That adventurous gypsy spirit has endured through the decades, and we did a similar trip to Alaska in 1967 when the ALCAN Highway was still a winding, dirt road.

I was really lucky to live in Switzerland for eight months in 1968 with my family. We missed five months of school but got a superior education by visiting castles, museums, and ancient ruins. As a college student without much money in the 1970s, I hitchhiked up and down the Eastern Seaboard and the Canadian Maritimes.

COASTAL SYMPHONY, 2009 ● 50¾ x 37 inches (128.9 x 94 cm) ● Hand-painted and commercial cotton, acrylic paints, oil sticks; fused appliqué, free-motion quilted ● Photo by artist

Patricia Gould

THE WAITING, 2009 ● 52½ x 34 inches (133.4 x 86.4 cm)
Cotton and polyester fabrics, acrylic paints; fused appliqué,
free-motion quilted ● Photo by artist

A PAIR OF KINGS, 2009 ● 34 x 43 inches (86.4 x 109.2 cm)
● Hand-painted jacquard silk, acrylic paints, oil sticks; fused
appliqué, free-motion quilted ● Photo by artist

Fast-forward to 1983 when I met my husband, who also loves to travel. In addition to visiting 49 of the 50 states and all of the Canadian provinces, we have explored five other continents, including Antarctica. Many of the trips were cultural, and some were focused on wildlife, but most were a combination of the two. Russia was exciting in 1993, not long after the dissolution of the USSR. In 1989, we camped inside the Ngorongoro Crater in Tanzania, where we witnessed rhinos mating (such an uncommon sight that a World Wildlife Fund crew was filming it), and lions breathed on our tent during the night.

All my travels and the photographs I've taken to document my experiences have given me incredible inspiration for more works than I could ever complete in a lifetime. I've also acquired some interesting pieces of fabric to incorporate into my work.

Rocks and Water

My father took me fossil hunting in the Catskills when I was eight years old, and I fell in love with rocks. This is another thing I share with my husband; we cherish our rock collections, and we love the hunt. In addition to collecting these treasures, I pay tribute to them in my landscapes. Rocks are so interesting to portray; they have subtle nuances of color, wonderful texture, and when you emphasize their shadows, you add so much three-dimensionality to the scene.

I still love to visit the ocean—not for the thrill of swimming but to take in the life-affirming qualities of the seashore. Waterfalls, lakes, and rivers are also favorite subjects of mine. The most dramatic ocean photographs I've taken are from Antarctica, a place of pristine air and water, frightening winds and waves, and massive, ancient icebergs that display the most incredible range of blue colors.

New Mexico

Since 1993 I have lived in New Mexico. Unlike the rest of my family, who still live on the ocean, I fell in love with the high desert back in the 1980s. Once I spent time in the Four Corners region of the United States, I realized how much I hated humidity, biting insects, and crowds of people. After my husband and I moved to New Mexico, rocks become a major inspiration for my fiber art. The incredible skies here are very strong influences on my work and enhance the beauty of the unique rock formations.

Photography

Photography is another passion of mine, and I almost majored in it in college until I took ceramics and fell in love with the tactile experience. I've been photographing the world since the age of eight, and when I have taught landscape fiber art classes, I try to get the students to see the world through that little viewfinder, as I do.

I work from photographs: about 80 percent of the time I portray an actual scene, and for the other 20 percent, I use photographs as ideas for an imaginary scene. Years ago, I would draw a full-scale rendering and create templates for the entire piece. I no longer work that way; instead, I do a rough sketch on paper and merely suggest what the scene will look like. I then paint the skies and water (if a coastal scene) using acrylics for cotton fabrics or dyes for silk fabrics and use paint sticks for added depth and realism.

I pile up mounds of various fabrics I like and start cutting pieces to apply to the scene. I frequently critique the work on my design wall as it progresses and often add more paint or inks for more realistic rendering and details. Once the top is finished, I'll quilt and do thread painting on it for more texture and detail. I often also go back in after the stitching and add more detail or shading with inks or paints.

Lately, I've begun to quilt the skies or water before adding in the other elements, as that is physically so much easier. I've also begun to do some heavily thread-painted elements, such as foliage or birds, creating them separately and then appliquéing them on later so that they lay flat on the work.

Hand-Painted Fabrics

I find that working with fabric and thread is a much greater challenge than simply painting realistic and semi-realistic landscapes, especially when rendering the effects of chiaroscuro (light and shadow). I also like the tactile experience of handling the fabrics that you don't get by applying paint to canvas.

MOONRISE, NORTH RIM, 2009 ● 46 x 63 inches (116.8 x 160 cm) ● Hand-painted and commercial cotton, acrylic paints, ink; fused appliqué, free-motion quilted ● Photo by artist

When I began creating landscapes in 1993, all I used were commercial fabrics. I slowly found myself enhancing those fabrics with paints and dyes. After taking a silk-painting class, I was confident enough to create some whole-cloth painted works. The decision as to what is the best way to say what I am trying to convey dictates how I will approach each piece. Much of that depends on how much texture I want in the work; the more texture I want, the more types of fabrics and paints I will use. If I want a flatter, more graphic-looking image, I'll use a smaller array of fabrics or create a whole-cloth piece.

I'm also trying to use up my huge stash of fabric, so I often over-paint. For *Coastal Symphony*, the base fabric began life as a pale green calico-type fabric. I painted the fabric and applied paint sticks only to find that it was too green, so I went back and painted another coat of blue on the back. I collect batiks that I think have rock-like personalities, but find that adding shading to them with paint sticks really brings them to life.

Whispering a Tribute

Although I am not an artist with an "in-your-face" type of message, I don't intend for my work to be merely pretty pictures. My voice is whispering a tribute to the incredible beauty to be found in both the subtle and violent forces of nature, those only touched by the hand of humans on rare occasions. I portray my subjects as if they were asking to me to reveal their messages to the world. My fiber pieces are dramatic portraits of Earth, and I hope to draw the viewers into these scenes to share the exhilaration I feel and to cherish the wonders of the planet we call home. I'm really thrilled when people ask about the place I have portrayed, since I would like my work to inform and inspire people to become better caretakers of the planet.

BLUE CATHEDRAL, 2001 ● 37 x 55 inches (94 x 139.7 cm) ● Hand-painted cotton and taffeta, cotton, satin, polyester; machine and hand appliquéd, free-motion quilted ● Photo by artist ● Marbaum Collection, Estate of Hilary Morrow Fletcher

PETRIFIED LOG RHYTHMS, 2008 ● 30 x 32 inches (76.2 x 81.3 cm) ● Hand-painted and commercial cotton, hand-marbled cotton and paper, organza; fused appliqué, free-motion quilted ● Photo by artist ● Collection of the New Mexico Arts Division, Art in Public Places Program, Curry County Fairgrounds, Clovis, New Mexico

● Patricia Gould

textures

MARY ARNOLD ● ROCK GARDEN, 2010 ● 48 x 41 inches (121.9 x 104.1 cm) ● Batiks
and hand-dyed fabric, ink; hand appliquéd, machine quilted ● Photo by Mark Frey

DENISE LINET ● MEADOW, 2009
● 31 x 39 inches (78.7 x 99.1 cm)
Hand-dyed and -painted cotton;
screen-printed, Xerox lithography,
machine pieced and fused, machine
and hand stitched ● Photo by artist

ELIZABETH BRIMELOW ● SOLE BAY, 2008 ● Each panel, 13½ x 88 inches (34.3 x 223.5 cm) ● Silk, cotton, wool-linen fabric; hand and machine stitched, direct and reverse appliquéd, fused, screen-printed, hand dyed, knotted ● Photo by Michael Wicks

MARTHA COLE ● FIRST TURNING, 2007 ● 64½ x 48½ inches (163.9 x 123.2 cm) ● Digital image on polyester fabric, archival pigment-based inks, fabric paints, assorted threads, unbleached cotton, polyester batting, whole cloth; free-motion stitched ● Photo by Carolyn Pihach

TIZIANA TATEO ● RIVER PEARLS, 2009 ● 52 x 58 inches (132.1 x 147.3 cm) ● Cotton, abaca tissue, puff paint, rayon, cotton threads; photo transfer, machine embroidered and quilted ● Photo by artist

ROSEMARY CLAUS-GRAY ●
RIVER OATS, 2005 ● 22½ x 19¼ inches
(57.2 x 48.9 cm) ● Scrim, hemp; needle
felted, couched, embroidered ● Photo
by artist ● Courtesy of the Artfully
Framed Gallery, Poplar Bluff, Missouri

KATHLEEN MCCABE
● BARREL CACTUS, 2010 ●
16 x 16 inches (40.6 x 40.6 cm) ●
100% cotton, commercial fabrics;
fused, machine, and reverse appliquéd, machine quilted ● Photo by
Phil Imming

CAROL WATKINS ● PRAIRIE RAINBOW, 2009 ● 34 x 42 inches (86.4 x 106.7 cm) ● Photographs, cotton, acrylic paint, thread; digital processes, inkjet printed, free-motion embroidered ● Photo by Ken Sanville

ABOUT THE AUTHOR

Martha Sielman is the author of *Masters: Art Quilts, Volumes 1* and *2* (Lark Books, 2008 and 2011). Sielman is Executive Director of Studio Art Quilt Associates, Inc. (SAQA), the world's largest art quilt organization dedicated to advancing art quilting as a fine-art medium. Her career in art quilts began in 1988, when she learned to quilt, and has included more than 20 years of work as a professional artist, author, lecturer, curator, juror, and arts administrator.

Since joining SAQA as its Executive Director in 2004, Sielman has witnessed the explosive growth of art quilting, as well as growing interest in art quilts as a legitimate and collectible fine-art medium. The increasing popularity of art quilting is evidenced by SAQA's 2,900 members from over 30 countries, the explosion of art quilt exhibits around the globe, the blockbuster success of the *Masters: Art Quilts* books and exhibits, and SAQA's receipt in 2010 of a Visual Arts grant from the National Endowment for the Arts.

Sielman has written articles about art quilts for *Quilting Arts Magazine*, *Machine Quilting Unlimited*, and *Fiberarts Magazine*, and has appeared on the HGTV show *Simply Quilts*. She was curator for both the *Masters: Art Quilts 1* and *Masters 2* exhibitions, which traveled extensively in the United States and abroad, and she served as a juror for the 2009 NICHE Awards and for Pushing the Limits: New Expressions in Hooked Art.

Sielman lives in Storrs, Connecticut, with her husband, five children, and two cats.

ACKNOWLEDGMENTS

I would like to thank Ray Hemachandra for helping me conceive and refine the concepts for the *Art Quilt Portfolio* series. Ray's thoughtful questions and creative insights were the starting point for an incredible journey. Valerie Shrader has been a wonderfully supportive and discerning editor. It's infinitely comforting to hear her upbeat voice on the phone—no deadline crisis is insurmountable. And nothing would have gotten done without the critical organizational help of Dawn Dillingham, Julie Hale, and assistant editor Thom O'Hearn, who kept hundreds of images and contracts straight. Finally, I could not have written any of this without the loving support of my husband, David, and my kids: Ben, Katie, Daniel, Lucy, and Jonathan. Thanks for letting me have the time to write and not have to cook dinner, clean, or attend every single basketball game.

Feature Artist Index

Gallery Artist Index

Thirteen Ways of Looking at a Blackbird